The
GODDESS
BADE ME
DO IT!

To Claudia

May the Goddess
bless you and keep
you for the rest of your days

Love
Lady Loreon

Temple of Isis
ISIS OASIS SANCTUARY
20889 Geyserville Avenue
Geyserville, California 95441
707-857-ISIS (4747)
isis@isisoasis.org
www.isisoasis.org

THE GODDESS BADE ME DO IT—LOREON VIGNÉ.
ISBN 0-9779481-0-2

10 9 8 7 6 5 4 3 2 1

Designed by Alian Design www.aliandesign.com

The GODDESS BADE ME DO IT!

THE AUTOBIOGRAPHY OF THE
RT. REVEREND LOREON VIGNÉ,
ARCH PRIESTESS OF ISIS

TEMPLE OF
ISIS

Dedication

I dedicate this book to Lady Olivia Robertson of the Fellowship of Isis who has been my mentor and an inspiration not only to me, but to so many others on the path of the Goddess.

I wish to thank all who have become clergy in The Temple of Isis as well as those who have inspired me to write this book.

Lastly, I want to thank those who have helped me with the technical aspects of creating this book... The Goddess Bade Me Do It!

If the Goddess is calling you to be of service
you may contact the Temple of Isis at the
ISIS OASIS SANCTUARY
20889 Geyserville Avenue
Geyserville, California 95441
707-857-ISIS (4747)
isis@isisoasis.org
www.isisoasis.org

Table of Contents

Introduction

When I tell my life story, listeners are amazed at the coincidences that permeate the various twists and turns I have taken. I realize that I have experienced a great many aspects of what a human being is about, all in order to be worthy of the title of Priestess. I am happy to share the lessons I have learned in this unusual life.

Although I didn't realize it at the time, Isis, the ancient Egyptian Goddess of Nature, became my mentor, and perhaps even my mother, at the tender age of six. It was she who later prompted me to create Isis Oasis and to develop and expand it for twenty-five years. In her honor I continue to do her work. I believe the name and spirit of the Goddess Isis must be kept alive in this modern world.

Isis is a feminine deity with magical powers. She is known today as Mother Earth and certainly is not as loved and respected as when Isis was honored in ancient Egypt. The Temple of Isis is part of a larger movement that is bringing that reverence for Nature, as personified by the Goddess Isis, once again to the forefront of human understanding.

Those who believe that there is an imbalance in all areas of this contemporary era will do well to connect with the Goddess.

So, here I present to you the story that brought me to this place. I relate the many journeys that have been prelude to my life's final denouement. As I re-remember the various events that are woven into the fabric of my web of existence, I can see the images so clearly, as if no time at all had passed. They are precious recollections, each bringing further understanding of the position in which I now find myself.

I have now grown old and have manifested, with the aid of the Goddess, a fair amount of opulence throughout my long life. I know it is my destiny to leave a legacy of bringing the Temple of Isis back into prominence. It is an ancient concept, perhaps older than any other belief system on the planet: the return to the divine feminine and the expansion of freedom of thought, free of dogma. I coined the word "catma" to express the qualities of the Temple of Isis. A cat is independent and balanced, loving and gentle.

At Isis Oasis we create a world of our own within the world that exists outside. We surround ourselves with other creatures of Nature, with art and beauty, and with the conviction that what we have created here must be shared freely with others. The ancient tree that is the centerpiece of this amazing ten acres of land is a source of wonder and wisdom. I know my path is to make certain that this vision is carried on beyond me to continue to expand like the roots of the sacred tree.

May you enjoy the romp through the passages of my time on Earth with me, and may your life, too, take turns that will lead you to awaken your dreams and live your passion!

Loreon holding a Goddess Hathor Sistrum at convocation, 2005

CHAPTER I ———————————————————————

The Cocoon

*L*uminous moments occur in one's life that often
have the power of creating transformation. Most of
us remember times in our lives that were painful.
These incidents are stored magically in the files of
our mind to be recalled when it is appropriate to
recount them.

My first experience of this kind took place
when I was five, sitting in a rocking chair on the
wide verandah of an old house in White Plains, New
York. I was cutting out *Gone With the Wind* paper
dolls, carefully clipping the tabs on the voluminous
green dress Scarlet O'Hara had made out of
draperies. The dress was colored to look like soft
velvet, tied at the waist with a thick rope decorated
at both ends with golden tassels. My parents had

never taken me to a movie, so I had not seen *Gone With the Wind* and was too young to read it, but the paper dolls intrigued me. I was able to clearly imagine the rich drama they seemed to portray.

I was concentrating so intently on the intricacies of cutting this exotic garment perfectly that I did not notice that the rungs of my rocking chair had become stuck under the railings of the porch. Upon realizing my predicament, I tried my best to extricate myself, but instead flipped head over heels and landed upside down with the little scissors I had been using lodged in the center of my right palm.

I looked in horror at the stigmata of the small scissors imbedded in my bleeding hand. I remember crying out in pain, which prompted my mother to come to investigate. Her red hair was tightly wound in curlers and her furrowed brow looked angry and annoyed. There was no sign of kind concern, only blame for my clumsiness.

With a fearful expression, she pulled the scissors from my bloody hand and we went to the hospital where my wound was dressed and I was given some medication that caused me to be very woozy. I was taken home with instructions to lie down for the remainder of the day.

My room was tiny, actually an oversized closet. It was the only room of my own I was ever to have as long as I lived with my parents. I lay in my small bed in a state of euphoria just above the threshold of sleep. Suddenly, before my dreamy eyes, I observed a phenomenon of nature.

There was a jar on a table beside my bed which contained a cocoon that I had collected in the woods behind the house. I was fascinated by insects and would watch the ants, spiders, butterflies, and beetles with total awe and admiration, but I had never witnessed the marvel of nature I was about to observe.

The cocoon, which looked like a ball of spun honey, began to open. Slowly, out of it emerged a fantastically huge and colorful moth. (I learned later it was a Cecropian moth.) It waved its feathery feelers, but its wings, glistening and seemingly moist, were motionless for what felt like a very long time. Slowly it began to flap these beautifully designed wings. I could see its furry body and delicate black legs holding onto the twig where the cocoon was attached.

After awhile, I remember thinking that I must do something with the moth, now perfectly poised on its perch in the jar. My room contained a gold bird cage with very narrow bars. I picked up the twig with the moth still clinging on it, not yet ready to fly, and sequestered it in the golden cage.

In the evening, I placed the cage, with the beautiful moth inside, on the porch where the accident with the scissors had occurred. When the effects of the drug I had been given began wearing off, I returned to visit the moth and was amazed to see there was another moth outside the cage, an exact replica of the one inside.

They were clinging to the golden bars and flapping their huge wings directly opposite each other. (This was a mystery to me then, but later I learned about the scent the female moth gives off to attract the male moth, even over great distances.)

The next morning I went to visit the moths again. I was saddened to find that both moths had vanished, In their place was a multitude of what I now know were eggs, attached like shiny beads to the golden bars.

This moth memory, the witness of the mating and disappearance, had a profound effect on me. The observance of these and other natural phenomena has served as a guiding force throughout my life. These wonders I attribute to the ancient Egyptian Goddess Isis, mother of all Nature. You may know her as Mother Earth.

The transformative emergence of the moth out of its cocoon let me understand that I would take my own path in life. Even at that early age, I became detached from my parents and their expectations of me. Witnessing this beautiful moth suddenly find its identical mate, then vanish from the golden cage, leaving behind hundreds of tiny jewels, each one of which would become a beautiful moth itself one day, instructed me as well: I sensed that my own unique path would lead me into an abundance of magical experiences. And so it has been.,

I was born in Manhattan, New York, on June 8, 1932 at 8:15 p.m.. My mother named me Loralee and my middle name was June. It was the height of the Great Depression, but my father still had a job. He was working in Harlem as a salesman in a men's clothing store. He had come from London, England as a lad by stowing away on a ship. He had intense blue eyes and dark hair and was a ringer for the actor, David Niven. His name was David, too. He and my mother, whose name was Frieda, met at a dance in Manhattan and wed young.

While I was still in the womb my mother found out that my father had been having sex with a black woman and assumed he had contracted a social disease. I'm sure she went ballistic. I was told this lurid story when I was around forty by my Aunt Jean, and it didn't surprise me. I had always associated my mother with extreme unhappiness, and, of course, we know now that what the mother thinks and feels affects the fetus.

On this same visit with Aunt Jean, I asked about a memory I had while I was still a baby in a crib. I knew somehow my father had lost his job and a feeling of insecurity overcame me. I witnessed my mother having a tantrum when she heard the news, yelling and screaming, a behavior I always associated with her. I described to my aunt the surroundings that I remembered. She had been living with us at that time and told me I was around two years old.

It's quite amazing to realize that this kind of understanding is possible at so tender an age. This incident undoubtedly significantly traumatized me, and as my personality developed I became a rather shy and withdrawn child, often wishing I might belong to a different family.

When I was around 4 years old we moved from the city to the suburbs of White Plains on the old Boston Post Road. It was the only time our family lived in a real house, even though it was a duplex. My sister Caryl, who was six years my senior, had her own friends, but a young girl just my age lived downstairs. Her name was Joan Graabe and she was very beautiful. Next door, in an exactly matching duplex, lived two other families, each with young boys also around our age. Their names were Jimmy and Wolfgang. These were the first playmates I remember.

All of these families happened to be of German origin. It was the time that Hitler was surfacing in Germany and my mother, being of Jewish descent, warned me that these children were my enemies. This caused me a lot of anxiety as I really enjoyed my young friends, and in no way could I imagine they might be foes. I ignored her, of course, and went on with my friendships, playing marvelous games with the three of them.

I was a cute child and my mother dressed me like a doll. She liked to take pictures of me, insisting I pose in very particular positions. She would always try to arrange my hair, but I did not like her to touch me and would recoil and react violently at her attempts to control me.

On the fourth of July she entered me in a pageant. She dressed me in a Hawaiian costume

with a grass skirt and colorful lei. I was strumming
a ukulele which Aunt Jean had given me. I was elated
when I won, but the prize consisted of $10 worth
of groceries. This did not excite me because what
I really wanted was a doll. Joan Graabe had lots of
dolls and many furry teddy bears that lined shelves in
her room. The only dolls I was given were some small
wooden dogs that were decorations from the window
of the store where my father worked.

I dreamed of having a real doll of my own. I made
a fuss about this and my mother agreed to get me a doll,
in exchange for the food that I, in effect, had provided
the household by winning the prize. It was a Shirley
Temple doll, with adorable curls and a beatific smile. I
was very happy and wanted to show it to my playmates,
but my mother said I absolutely must not. The doll had
to stay inside and be safe and protected.

I remember meeting my little friends beside the
house and loudly declaring that I hated my mother. I
was overheard by my older sister who was in her room
above us. She looked out the window and admonished
me for saying negative things about my mother. She said
I should not talk that way. I can feel what it was like even
now, looking up at her in her lofty perch. My friends
must have agreed with her and began to shun me, which
made me sad.

Perhaps my parents were feeling sorry for me
being so alone, for they took me to the animal pound
in town and allowed me to pick out two puppies
that I could play with. I called them Dot and Dash,

and of course I loved them dearly. Then, after only about a week, I was told that my mother was allergic to them and they had to go back to the pound. I can remember that day and the feeling of extreme misery.

I was never again allowed to have a pet, yet I persisted in my dream of being friends with an animal. I knew there were some feral cats around, having seen them now and then while I was sitting in a dogwood tree I loved to climb. One day I discovered a feral cat living in the high weeds in the field beside our house. I remember running after him through the tall grasses, queen anne's lace, and black-eyed susans, getting soaking wet from the morning dew. Eventually I succeeded in catching that plain gray cat and managed to tame him enough so he would come and sit on the porch of the old house with me, though he was never allowed inside.

Across the field from the house was an amazing old mansion that was all boarded up. There was lots of foliage around the house that I admired, especially a mulberry tree I could stand inside of and completely hide within. There was also a dogwood tree and magnolias that I could climb to sit among the flowers. The lily of the valley and lilac bushes bloomed in spite of no one caring for them.

The house was full of mystery because it had been owned by the Quimby sisters, who had died suddenly in an accident. A marvel to us children, this house made a deep impression on me—perhaps my first step into the world of the occult. Though

I dreamed of entering it, I never got up enough courage to actually do that, though behind it was a barn where I found lots of memorabilia: old photos, an ancient zither and other odd objects, which I carted back to the attic at my house.

I spent the summer hours walking in the woods behind our house where there was a mound of sticks made into what looked like a hovel that was said to house a hermit. I was always careful to avoid this hut, for I feared to meet him, only imagining who he could be.

I loved nature and found solace from my dysfunctional family and lack of friends by communing with the birds, bees, and frogs that surrounded the house. I remember feeding the ants peanuts and watching as they gathered their forces to take the offering into their lair.

Naturally, when it was announced that we were going to move I became distraught. I was in kindergarten and I remember when all the other children were drawing pictures of houses with the sun shining and everything looking bright, I created a picture of nighttime with a black background in a blizzard of white snow. (I always had to be different.) Having moved from an apartment to this house with all its wonderful grounds where I could get in touch with the Earth, I could not understand why we would have to move to another apartment house where concrete would surround us.

I was told that my father did not like shoveling

coal to keep us warm in winter. This was really the only time I could talk to him, for he was not often home. I remember sitting with him as he engaged in this simple act of stoking the furnace and being content to observe the flames dancing on the black coals, feeling somehow taken care of by my father as I never did before or afterward, for his work as a haberdasher engrossed him completely.

So, shortly after, there I was in another apartment house. There was nothing anyone could do to make me happy. I refused to play with other children in the nearby park that looked so very sterile. A sandbox and swings on a green lawn didn't inspire me and I refused to go there. I shared a room with my sister, who was often not home, and spent much of my time with my paper dolls. My only real doll was the one I was not allowed to play with. My mother made a hula skirt for that doll and one day dressed me in the costume just like it and had me pose in the exact position of the doll.

Today this photograph brings back the sadness that settled into my psyche as a very disappointed and deprived little girl. Still, I had had the moth experience and knew that I, too, could be transformed. I could begin to fly and someday I would have a mate who would magically find me.

I would often dance, but only when no one was around. Once when I was dancing I saw my parents peeking at me from around the corner. Probably they noticed I had some talent in this direction and surprisingly they offered to enroll me in a school for ballet.

I remember going to get my pink ballet slippers and my multicolored tutu trimmed in gold, and how this sparked my life into something more than the mundane. I adored the dance class, but for some reason I was put with older, more experienced children and I often felt overwhelmed. Still, I dreamt of being a *prima ballerina*.

The ballet lessons continued until we moved again, this time to Teaneck, New Jersey, as Father had been transferred to a men's clothing store in Hackensack. In school I was the teacher's pet, so leaving that school was another trauma since I had such a good relationship with this teacher. She inspired me to dance in a program in the auditorium of the school. I can remember that performance vividly. I did all the choreography myself to the music of the "Waltz of the Flowers" and my picture was put in the local paper.

In Teaneck we were once again to live on the top floor of an apartment building, the only one in Teaneck at the time. I was not to have ballet lessons, for there was no place in town where they were given, according to my mother. I began to concentrate on my abilities to draw and sing instead, and won a poster contest given by the Red Cross. I also sang a solo number in a school program.

I loved to read and my favorite books were about mythology. The story of the Princess who lived on Glass Mountain from *East of the Sun and West of the Moon* became a script for my life. Of course, I came to understand this only later, when I looked at how distant from others I often made myself. No one could touch me, and above all I must always be different.

It was about this time that my mother tried to commit suicide by locking herself in the bathroom and drinking iodine. I can remember this, but my sister Caryl does not. She has almost no memory at all of our family life and thinks I dwell on the unpleasant aspects far too much. Perhaps, but for me there was little that was enjoyable about our family.

The school I attended was just at the end of the block. Maybe being a ballerina had enhanced my ability to be friendly, for this time I got to know quite a few of the children in my class in the fifth and sixth grades. As the school roll-taker, which I would do each morning, I learned everyone's names, and found I enjoyed it. I also discovered I could be humorous and often even gregarious.

My teacher, Mr. Swan, who was also the principle of the school, was quite handsome, wore tweeds, smoked a pipe, and was tremendously compassionate and kind. Everyone liked him, especially me, as he was responsible for my having the opportunity to create a huge mural in the sixth grade. I was allowed to skip classes to work on this project in the gymnasium of the school. It depicted the United Nations that was beginning to be formed in those days. I painted a long table with both men and women seated at it in the costumes of their country of origin. I did research at the library to make my mural as authentic as possible and was quite pleased with the work. Perhaps this presaged my desire to create large projects in the future.

One day I got to school to learn that one of the students died. Her name was Anna Neagle, the most gorgeous girl in the class. She had a heart condition and sadly succumbed. Mr. Swan arranged for all the class to walk to the funeral parlor. There she was, with her hair in long curls carefully arranged within her satin lined casket, surrounded by flowers and looking very angelic, This was my first death experience. When we returned to school, it was the day for having our eyes tested, but by then most of us were teary and red -eyed.

It was war time and the Nazis were in full swing. I collected old cans for the war effort and sold stamps and bonds in a booth in front of my father's store in Hackensack on Saturdays.

Alas, instead of going on to the high school where my sister went and having some continuity, we were to move again, this time to Los Angeles, California, where some members of my parents' families had already migrated. Some of the kids in my school in Teaneck thought I might become a movie star, and even I began to think that could be possible

It was a long journey in the car with four of us. Mostly I remember the Burma Shave signs along the highways. Once we arrived, each of us stayed with different parts of the family until my parents could find a place to live. For two months we stayed in Venice in a nice house with a piano that I adored trying to play. I started at a school that was accessed by a wonderful old street car.

Then, as soon as I was feeling comfortable about being there, I had to change schools, for my parents moved us into a tiny apartment in a different part of the city, where I was to be ensconced during the rest of my junior high and high school years. My sister had gone off to Stanford University, which in those days was somewhat affordable, though she worked her way through with the help of our parents. My mother sold vacuum cleaners door to door to assist with the finances. I slept in the kitchen dinette and suffered, needing my own space.

In high school I started painting in oils and made an arrangement to use a garage in the rear of the apartment complex to set up my own studio. From babysitting money I purchased an enormous easel from a well-known artist and began to envision myself a painter. To outfit my studio, I made tables and chairs from old barrels being discarded by the delicatessen down the street. There I spent my time after school.

I never lunched with the crowd, but instead spent that time in the art room. Mrs. Mellini, my art teacher, was my savior. I never dressed like the other girls, preferring sandals to saddle shoes. One thing I did do that was social was sing in the chorus. I enjoyed the harmony of the large group and could sing a pretty good soprano.

As a teen I took a number of jobs: babysitting, sales jobs, and then as an artist's model for several woman artists, which only enhanced my idea of being an artist myself.

When I neared graduation I found myself in an interesting situation: I had not taken academic courses such as my sister chose, and so college was not an option for me, but my grades in the courses I did take put me at the top of the class. As a result, I was offered a scholarship to either an art school or a music school. I choose the art school.

As I look back today, at my now-advanced age, I am astonished at how many reversals I have made from my roots. Often those who have trials find themselves metamorphosed by making up for that which was lacking. As you shall see, I morphed into a person who, from not being allowed any pets, now has over twenty exotic cats (ocelots, serval cats, jungle cats, and bobcats) and over one hundred beautiful and colorful birds. Coming from having no room of my own and sleeping in the kitchen dinette, I now have several homes and over fifty rooms. I even have a whole room just for my clothes, including a costume closet, whereas as a child I just had hand-me-downs from my big sister. Today, I have my own theatre with a big screen and a huge collection of films to show. Among the films I treasure most is, of course, *Gone with the Wind*.

Perhaps most unusual is that I find myself a

Priestess in the Temple of Isis, a recognized church that is resurrecting the ancient Egyptian traditions. I am also an Arch Priestess in the International Fellowship of Isis, founded by Lady Olivia Robertson and her brother Lord Strathloch from their home at Castle Clonegal, Enniscorthy, Ireland.

The International Fellowship of Isis has thousands of members all over the world. These honors are most unusual, for I had no spiritual upbringing and as a young girl declared myself an agnostic.

I emerged from my cocoon, slowly at first, like the moth in the jar, and soon learned to create magic, both with my art and with my ability to manifest beyond my wildest imagination.

Loralee in her pink ballet slippers and tutu, age 9

Loralee with her two puppies Dot & Dash

Loralee with her only doll, being posed by her mothe, age 7

Loralee at her high school, age 16

The Emergence

I recall my first day at Kahn Institute of Art in Beverly Hills. I was filled with expectation. I had gotten on the bus in some artistic outfit I had dreamed up, carrying a fishing basket for a purse (having always to be different!). Perhaps, like a female moth, I was summoning another of the opposite sex, for on that same bus was a handsome young artist whom I quickly met at the school. His name was Frank. He showed a lot of interest in me, which I found very flattering.

When I graduated high school, I was still a virgin, although most of the girls I knew were not. Even though Frank and I got very close, I continued to remain chaste. Frank was a practicing Catholic and was very much in control of himself.

When my parents met him, he was wearing a large cross and this did not sit well with them. They protested my friendship with Frank, so thereafter we would meet in secret.

I would often go out painting with a group of students who were mostly men. I really enjoyed their camaraderie and had never had such a wonderful time as when we would set up our easels and paint for the afternoon, then eventually go somewhere to have marvelous discussions about art, politics, or religion. This was the bohemian life I sought.

When the school was out for the summer, my father requested the Kahn Institute *not* renew my scholarship. He did not want me being around Frank or the other artists who went to the school. I was too young, he said.

I was miserable and angry with my father's actions. I don't remember how I spent my summer, except that Frank and I drifted apart. I got a portfolio of my artwork together and managed to get another scholarship at a different art school that was in a rather unsavory part of town. The whole place was somewhat funky, so different from Kahn Institute in Beverly Hills, where movie stars went to study art. This was true Bohemia.

In the drawing class there was a board propped on a bench with wonderful drawings on it, but no one was there. Later, when I met the young man who made the drawings, I became as enamored of him as I was of his artwork. When he asked me to go out, I readily agreed.

His name was Dion Vigné. He was a very romantic figure. Dion wrote poetry as well as creating amazing art and he was having a show at a well-known gallery when I met him. His paintings were extremely non-objective and contemporary and everyone seemed to think he had a wonderful future in the art world.

His family was interesting, too. His father was a well-known Mexican actor and director, Emelio Fernandez, but he had his mother's stage name, Vigne. His father had never been on the scene, so his mother was clearly his guiding force. Dorothy was a beautiful woman, an intellectual, and ever so different from my own mother. Dion's stepfather was a cellist who taught music and played in chamber concerts. Their simple apartment was so interesting to me, filled as it was with books and art and music.

It was inevitable that I should fall in love with Dion. Once again a problem arose when my parents detected his Mexican origin, but they would not stop me this time. I was eighteen when, after a fantastic party Dion and I attended in Malibu, I lost my virginity. We were feeling very high, having quite a lot of alcohol and maybe a little marijuana. I can remember Dion and I looking into each other's eyes and knowing that our destiny was to be together. It was a very strong, compelling feeling. That night, upon returning to the apartment where I lived with my family in cramped quarters, I knew I would have

to figure out a way to leave. I needed my freedom.
I would no longer be part of their narrow world.
I was now a woman!

To make a further break I shortened my name
and was now called Lora.

I found an ad in the paper for a live-in *au pair*
near the California School of Art that I attended. It
was my opportunity to leave home. I washed dishes
and cared for the two children when the family was
out. This family did not make much of an impression
on me. It is hard to remember them today. I suppose
I was staying focused on my artwork at school and on
Dion. There were some good teachers at the school
and I learned as much as I could. Being engrossed in
art, as I was there, has always made me happy.

When the year was up at the school, I decided
to get a job and my own apartment. I had always
admired an area across from the Hollywood Bowl
called the French Village Apartments. It was filled
with artists and unusual structures for them to live
in. I sought a rental there. The space I could get was
just one room, but it had a fireplace and its own little
yard. I can remember innocently planting rows of
marijuana plants along the path. I was pretty naive
about the laws and was getting used to smoking it
with Dion. I thought it seemed to expand the mind,
an aspect I liked very much.

I would see Dion every other night and we
would visit interesting friends of his. They were
artists and experimental filmmakers in such places

as Topanga Canyon and the Hollywood Hills. Hollywood Boulevard was fascinating to be around then, and we would frequent the magazine stands, buying literary booklets typical of those days and attending foreign films at various locations around town. It was a memorable time and lasted a nice little while, until the French Village Apartments were to be torn down to make room for some monstrosity.

I was devastated at being displaced, but I found another place off the Sunset Strip with a larger room and kitchen and the necessary fireplace. This was near my work, for I had gotten a job painting fabrics in a place run by a very eccentric woman. It was rather fun and I learned a lot about production there.

It was the time of the Korean War and Dion, who was still living at home, got drafted into the Army. I spent a lot of my evenings painting and reading in my little apartment after work. The place was near the first art school I used to attend and one day I ran into Frank, This meeting seemed to me somewhat auspicious. He visited my apartment and I told him about Dion. It culminated in Frank and me making love, since we had never done that before. I think at the time I wanted to be sure that it was Dion whom I preferred, as I had been so fond of Frank, once upon a time. I thought I could determine my true preference through a sexual encounter. That evening I decided for certain that Dion was to be my mate. When Frank left, I told him this.

The next day a priest came to my door and

spoke to me. I cannot remember what it was about, but I think he wanted me to attend services at his church. I was certain that Frank had gone to him for confession and the priest followed up on it.

I was never interested in organized religion, other than to discuss it philosophically. I believed that people should choose their own path and I considered myself an agnostic. I had little or no religious background given to me by my family and never accepted the concept of Jews as being a race, as so many people seemed to think.

Interestingly enough, Frank had chosen Catholicism although it was not the religion of his family. This I found rather exotic, but sending a priest to see me was a little outrageous and demeaning of our friendship. I did not see Frank again after that.

My job with the fabric company ended when the factory closed down rather suddenly, so I found another job painting lamp bases. It was not as pleasing as the fabrics and rather hard work. Still, I could make my own way. Dion's friends came over to see me now and then. Once, when his friend Norman, a trombone player, was visiting, my father unexpectedly knocked on the door. I hid Norman in the kitchen until he left, for father would never understand even a platonic relationship. My parents had few friends and were very closed to most experiences in life.

After about six months in the army, Dion got

busted for pot, which was discovered in his locker. His mother came to his rescue, however, by going to Fort Ord, where he was stationed, and using her charms to impress his superiors. He got an honorable discharge and came back to be with me once again.

We determined to live together. We both got employment at Douglas Aircraft, and set up an apartment together. But neither of us was happy there and in a few months we decided to leave. We had heard of a great studio space in Pasadena. We went to see it and that was it. We gave up our jobs and moved into it to try to maintain our originality and artistic pursuits in this time of war and industrialism.

I got a job airbrushing and hand painting ceramics. I did this as piecework and, being very fast, soon was making pretty good money.

The studio we lived and did our artwork in was enormous, the whole top floor of what once had been a firehouse. It had tall windows, skylights, beamed ceilings and brick walls, and we created a very picturesque home. We started to work in ceramics here. We obtained a kiln and began making small figurines such as I was producing where I worked. We were moving toward a goal of having our own business.

One day Dion announced he was going to Mexico with some friends to score. I thought he meant for marijuana, which we smoked with his friends often. In those days you could purchase a hefty amount for a reasonable sum. Not as many young people where using it then as today. In those days, living together out of wedlock was also very frowned upon, whereas today most couples seem to do that to assure themselves that they are compatible.

In any case, Dion was gone on this excursion for a few days and I remained at home in the studio. I remember having an ominous feeling, as though something were about to happen. Dion returned, however, and I was happy to see that all had gone well. He was going to some people's house to deliver some of what he had purchased in Mexico. I decided to accompany him and called in sick from my job.

We drove to the home of these people in our little coupe and I soon found myself in the company of junkies. Dion had brought back heroin from south of the border.

I had once experienced that drug and found it not to my liking. I did not know the consequences, being fairly ignorant, but here I was with a group that was shooting up. I tried some again, just to see if I was missing something. Again I decided it was not for me. Dion and I left under the influence of the drug. He should never have been driving.

On the Pasadena Freeway, Dion must have nodded off at the wheel and ran head-on into a telephone pole. We were both thrown out of the car and I awoke on the freeway being given last rites by a minister. There was blood on my face. Soon we were taken by ambulance to a hospital on gurneys, side by side. I remember Dion holding my hand as the ambulance sped toward the hospital, proclaiming his love for me. He had broken his left arm and he was left-handed. It was a most traumatic scene, always to be remembered.

At the hospital we were separated and treated for our injuries. I had a cut across my nose that required a bunch of stitches. We had miraculously survived the crash, though the car was totaled. People from the newspapers came to get our picture as we lay in our hospital beds. When we later got the paper, we learned the police made up lurid tales about an artists' party pad filled with drugs. Yes, I had a mark on my arm and Dion had more than one. Before then, I really had not been aware that he was using heroin to any extent, but he had indeed journeyed down that road.

After we were treated, we were released, only to be booked by the police and put in jail. I could not believe this was happening to me. Soon I was in a cell with another woman, amazed at the conditions under which we were supposed to exist. I was only the more miserable because I feared for my looks. My face was bruised and the stitches were ugly, going across my nose and up very close to my eye. I also had a lot of bruises on my body from the accident.

The women in the prison were very consoling and kind and offered a certain camaraderie. Many were black and I can remember one girl who waited tables in the dining room carrying a huge serving platter on her head. I had never seen anything like that before. She walked so proudly and looked very strong and beautiful, with an amazing smile displaying gleaming white teeth.

At a certain time of day, everyone went to the yard for exercise. Here I ran into Gin, a girlfriend of Bob Burke, a close friend of Dion's. I had met her on occasion but did not know her well, so her appearance at this place surprised me. She was a hooker, which was something new to me. The whole jail scene was a nightmare, but in retrospect I have always said I was meant to experience the misery and hopelessness of being in jail, for without being there, one cannot understand what it is to go through the system.

After about five days we were to be arraigned and I was called into court. My parents were there. Dion's parents were there, also. Here we were to tell our story of what happened. Dion said he was entirely at fault. I was only nineteen at the time and I could have gone home with my parents, but I absolutely refused to do this, so I was returned to my cell.

After about ten days in jail, Dion's mother, Dorothy, raised bail and got us both out. She had also arranged for us to go to the Justice of the Peace then and there, in that very same building, and get married so no one could part us. That is how we entered the state of matrimony… not very romantic.

We returned to our firehouse studio to discover that it had been ransacked by the police. That night we even realized that we were being watched by detectives on the roof of the building next door. I guess they thought they could find a large stash of something if they watched us. It was a weird time. We were both healing from our wounds. I had lost my job because of this debacle. We had nothing left, not even a car.

Dion was sentenced to a year in jail and I prepared myself to live alone in that large space. Dorothy helped me by getting me a job with a gift manufacturer of plastic butterflies. They were metal forms dipped in a thin coat of plastic film and I would airbrush them, hand paint them, and hang them up to dry on a folding laundry rack. Soon the whole space of our giant studio was filled with these winged objects, each with an original design. Dorothy, would pick up these butterflies when she and I visited Dion on the weekends.

In addition, I was making ceramic objects in the kiln, and she helped to find a buyer for these at the gift mart. I was working really hard and saving money to purchase a car and pay Dion's parents back for the money they laid out for our release from jail.

I assumed that my parents had given me up for good now. I was a non-person for them, I thought, until one day my mother called and said she wanted to visit and stay over. During her visit she seemed to have softened her attitude and was trying to be understanding. She indicated she really cared about what I was going through and offered to help in some way.

The next day, when Dion's mother came, my mother left. Soon after that there was a knock on the door and I opened it to plain clothes detectives, who insisted on searching us and the place. I realized then that my mother had called them and set this up, thinking, no doubt, that Dorothy was bringing me some drugs. It was very embarrassing and distanced me from my mother even further.

Shortly afterwards, my mother died. She had cancer of the colon. I visited her in the hospital before she passed away, but I had certainly hardened my heart toward her and her unhappy and dissatisfied existence. I remember her as always in a state of hysteria. No doubt she had her reasons, for her life was bereft of the excitement and creativity she probably craved. Still, it was hard to forgive her way of treating me.

My father did not wish to see me or speak to me. The firehouse was my home, often alone, and the year dragged on. Dion wrote to me daily and I cherished his letters.

One night, I had gone to bed when I was awakened by one of Dion's old friends, a musician by the name of Ed Taylor. He thought he would just stop by and pay me a visit. This proved a very fortunate circumstance, for while we were talking we discovered that there was a fire downstairs and we called the fire department. Had he not chosen that evening to stop by, I might have burned to death in that studio, for there was only one way out and no fire escape. After that Ed became an important friend in my life.

Finally the year was almost over and Norman, another musician friend helped me purchase a very special car, a 1928 Ford pickup in mint condition. This is what we picked Dion up in on the day he was freed. Certainly, he was very pleased. It was a joyous occasion, for we had been apart for a year and this absence brought us even closer.

Once back together we resumed our lives with new vigor, especially the business of ceramics. We had a representative on Hollywood Boulevard who purchased our wares and sold them. This was such a good thing that we decided after a time to rent a factory in Azusa. Dion, having an honorable discharge from the Army, was able to get a GI loan on a house in nearby Covina. For awhile after we moved into this brand new home things seemed wonderful but suburban living did not exactly fit our life style. We were spending a lot of time in the factory and did not seem to be enjoying the house and really could not afford it either, as our money was constantly reinvested in the ceramic business.

One day my father came to visit us and at least was somewhat cordial. He now owned his own men's clothing business in Santa Monica called "The House of David." He had also gotten in trouble with the law, having to do with a government contract for uniforms and his brother had gone to jail for this and ended up in the same facility Dion was in. Once, when I was visiting Dion at the honor farm in Castaic, I saw my father, who was visiting his brother.

Maybe this was why he seemed more amiable. He might have begun to see things like this can happen to anyone.

We attempted to show him that we were trying like regular folks to make it. However, we were not actually doing very well. We had purchased a large kiln with the help of a friend, who put up collateral for a loan for us. This was the backbone of the factory. Our ceramic line consisted of small figurines of animals and another line of sophisticated bowls and vessels. It was hard to make ends meet after paying staff and all the costs of making molds and purchasing supplies, In addition, it was difficult to get everything fired at the factory, for it took eight hours for every load. We would have to go back late at night to turn off the kiln. If we were not there at the right time, everything would over-fire.

Dion would sometimes leave the house and not come back in time. I knew he was still using drugs. In jail he had learned about Cheracol, a cough medicine that contained codeine which one could purchase without a prescription. He had been using it on a regular basis, but a friend of his had gotten him on heroin again. I became concerned and wished it were not happening. It drained our money, which was much needed to carry on. So we decided to sell the house and move into the office space in the factory. At least here we could watch the kiln and get our products fired properly.

Life began to seem hopeless to me. I had chosen this man to live with. I seemed to have no family anymore and no friends of my own. I was living out in the boonies and did not drive. I relied on Dion for companionship and he was my helpmate in the work we had chosen to do.

Sometimes to get away we would drive up into the San Bruno Mountains near the factory where there was a wonderful bubbling stream. I would hunt butterflies for the collection I was building up. I also started an insect collection.

Occasionally we would go to Hollywood to make deliveries and see Dion's friends. There was Edmond Teske, who was an exuberant and interesting individual and well known photographer; Jim Whitney, an experimental film maker; Norman Shacker, a strange albino-looking person who played the trombone; Ed Taylor, the Dixieland jazz pianist; Wally Berman, the artist; Mel Bowman, who was making mobiles; Norman Rose, a rare book seller; Bob Burke, who worked in the studios on sets; Gerard Baldwin, who did animation work for the studios; and Herb Landegger, who was a jeweler and was the one who engaged Dion in drug-related activities that I was so opposed to.

As winter came, we got lots of Christmas orders. We had purchased a large amount of shipping boxes and they were stored alongside the factory, when the first rain of the the season came, quite unexpectedly. We were in our office bedroom when we heard the sounds of raindrops, so Dion got up and put the shipping materials inside so they would not get wet. We went back to sleep but a little while later awoke to the sound and smells of a fire!

I remember jumping up, completely nude, and running to the next room where the telephone was, not far from the now-raging fire, and calling the fire department. By the time they came, all was in flames and the entire factory was destroyed.

Dion had put the shipping boxes too near the hot kiln and they ignited. All that we had worked so hard for had been destroyed. The factory building was badly charred and all our ceramic equipment looked like burnt charcoal. I had just one dress to wear that smelled horribly of fire.

However, the small enameling kiln somehow survived. Our black cat, Noir, had been at the vet that evening having all his blood replaced. After paying all our bills, we had only twenty dollars left. What were we to do?

I had always wanted to live in San Francisco. Some of our friends had moved there, so we packed everything we had left in the old pick-up and headed north. When we arrived, we stayed with Ed Taylor, our piano playing friend, who had helped me survive the fire on the first floor of the old firehouse studio. He had an apartment in a wonderful Victorian building on a corner of Van Ness Avenue.

I miraculously got a job designing the window of a shop next door and that was how we got money together to rent the place in North Beach that was to be our residence for a long time.

It was 1957, the beginning of the Beatnik era, and we fitted the description. Dion and I and our black cat Noir rented a basement in an alley off Grant Avenue for $60 a month. It contained thirteen cubicles, a kitchen and one large room, plus a kind of foyer. There were no windows except way up high in the large room and in the kitchen, and there was only a half bath, so we would have sponge baths at the kitchen sink. We furnished it with wooden boxes we picked up in the alleyways in Chinatown. I got a job with Schwabacher Fry in the art department, and Dion found work at Flax's art supply store. Ed Taylor and Norman Rose moved in with us, each in their own cubicle, until we could afford to pay the entire rent.

We began to be more creative and produced silk screens of San Francisco, inspired by the beauty that we found here in this amazing city. At that time, everything about the city was so alive and vital. Everyone dressed up in San Francisco in those days, and I would spend my lunch hour buying materials to make my own clothes to enlarge my meager wardrobe. I enjoyed walking to and from my work on Market Street wearing gloves, high heels and even a hat, so that I might blend in. I often wore black tights that the folks at Schwabacher Fry thought quaint.

Looking back, life was pretty good then, with the promise of better things to come. I started to experiment with enamels using the little kiln that survived the fire, I was able to purchase supplies at my job. Dion went back to drinking Cheracol, which seemed to satisfy his habit and only cost one dollar a day. It did not seem to interfere in our relationship at all.

North Beach was very colorful, filled with great Italian eateries. We could dine in Chinatown at the many Chinese restaurants scattered between the wonderful shops of exotic merchandise from that far off land. The color and character of the area far outweighed what Southern California had offered. We were pleased that we had ended up in this happening place.

It's funny how an unpleasant event, like a fire that destroyed everything culminated in our rising like the phoenix and landing in an environment that suited us much more. Sometimes it seems that the worst misfortune that could possibly befall us might actually create a change in life that eventually sets us on a new and better path. Therefore, even though a situation seems devastating at first, if we look to the future, that which seemed so dark and negative will find a way to be something wonderful and positive. This lesson can alleviate much pain and suffering. I have used this attitude frequently in my life and it surely has helped to minimize depression.

*Frank and Lora in front of
Kann Institute of Art, 1949*

Lora in the firehouse studio, 1951

Lora alone in the studio with her cat "Noir", 1951

Dion Vigné, a romantic figure, 1950

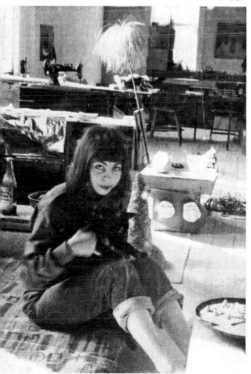

The Paint Pot

*N*orth Beach was getting a lot of notoriety in the papers. Herb Caen, the well-known journalist, had named the movement with the term "beatnik." One day, when Dion and I were going to dinner at the Paper Doll with Jordan Belson and his wife Jane, both experimental film makers, we passed a store front near Grant and Green that had a sign "For Rent" on it. It was just one store removed from the famous Bagel Shop. I looked into it, and bravely rented the store for $90 a month. I had decided to open an art supply store.

The place where I worked sold art supplies wholesale, so I had a great source. I arranged with them to get what I needed to begin. I planned to continue my job and open my store only in the evening.

No doubt there were shelves and counters in the store, for I cannot remember obtaining them, but I do remember a huge counter that had been thrown out in an alley downtown and I somehow managed to get it into that tiny shop. As it was fairly tall and very sturdy, I set up my little enameling kiln and had a lofty place to sit while making jewelry as I was waiting for customers. I was photographed working at this counter for the cover of a book called *I Am A Lover* by Jerry Stoll and Evan S. Connell, Jr. This book captured some of the rich images that one might see while visiting North Beach with suitable poetry.

On the first day of opening the shop which I named "The Paint Pot" I sold one bottle of black india ink. I had stocked pretty well, but not very deep, and although it took awhile to get started, it wasn't long before artists found their way to my counter. Eventually the Schwabacher Fry higher-ups realized that I might be competition and asked me to leave their employ. By then I was ready to work full time at The Paint Pot. Dion stayed on at Flax's and tried to stay out of my store, fearing to lose his job too if they knew of his connection with The Paint Pot.

I found it thrilling to be running my own little shop. It was just across the street from the Coffee Gallery, a very popular bar where lots of beatnik activity happened. I could see it, but did not participate. I worked hard keeping the shop going and doing my enamels that were now selling well to tourists and locals alike.

When time came for the second-ever Grant Avenue Street Fair, I got very involved. I was instrumental in organizing many new ideas like adding music and poetry. Crafts people and artists signed up at The Paint Pot and I got on radio and TV telling about its many promised wonders. The fair was a great success and it became the blueprint for other street fairs in many neighborhoods of San Francisco.

I also benefited nicely. From my booth in front of The Paint Pot I sold a lot of enamels, thousands of dollars worth. It was quite amazing. I was able to get more stock for the store and eventually move down the street to a larger location.

I was also beginning to sell the enamels to other stores. One of my clients was a tie company in the area called "Ernst Ties," famous for making the thinnest ties on the market. I made tie tacks and tie bars for them and got Dion a job doing a TV commercial for them with his 16 mm camera, He was immersed in the film world and did an experimental film called *North Beach* which was purchased by a patron of the arts who hung around the Beach. She saw some merit in it, even though, with its fast pace and strange-sounding background music, it put a lot of people off. Such was the way of experimental films.

We put on the Filmmaker's Follies at Fugazzi Hall in the late Fifties. This theatre had been neglected. Now it is the home of *Beach Blanket Babylon*, which has had great success. The Follies were fun and included lots of shenanigans, plus poetry, jazz, and films, of course.

Looking back, it is hard to believe I had time to juggle everything I took on.

I was doing some sewing in those days, designing clothes that were pretty off-beat. I remember doing a walk-on during the Follies wearing an outfit I called the "scavenger costume." It was a dress I made from a burlap sack and I also carried a large burlap bag inspired by the garbage men of the area. I wore a floppy black beret I had crocheted. Another design I was noted for was my fake fur clothes. I made tunics and shirts from this furry material, which I had sent from New York in large bolts.

All this I produced from one of the cubicles of the underground apartment that housed us in North Beach. Once in a while we had gatherings there, inviting the many characters we met while hanging around North Beach, but mostly we kept our noses to the grindstone seeking to enrich our lives.

Dion eventually quit his job to give himself full-time to art. I hired someone to run The Paint Pot so I could also work at home. I set up an area for making enamels more full scale, so I could fill the many orders I was receiving. Dion did a lot of the soldering and figuring out some of the technical aspects of the work, which I was not as good at.

He continued using Cheracol until one day it

became illegal to obtain without a prescription. This was a problem for him, as he was addicted to it. It was a problem for me too. I think he started to drink hard liquor around this time and probably began to purchase heroin, but I didn't notice much, I was so busy with my work.

I wanted to get out of the underground studio we had occupied for so long. We had enough money to buy a house and I found one in the Western Addition for only $1,500 down. It was in a black neighborhood and the realtor thought we were crazy to be interested in it. It was a two-story classic Italianate house with ten rooms and a garden. I was so thrilled to have my own home, and a Victorian at that! I was looking forward to fixing it up.

There was a lot to do to get the place painted and habitable. For awhile we slept in the living room on the first floor of the house. I was very happy, for I never imagined I could own such a fabulous house with a great many rooms and a yard.

When our cat Noir died, I decided to replace him with an ocelot. I found one in a newspaper ad and we brought him to the new house. I loved him dearly. He was the most beautiful creature I had ever seen and quite friendly to me and Dion. We built him some quarters in the house where he could make his way to a small outbuilding and he was also let out in the yard through a cat door we provided for him.

One morning I discovered a letter which had fallen out of Dion's shirt pocket. It was written to him by a women and it indicated they were having an affair. I was devastated. Even though I might be considered a beatnik, I still was very mainstream in my feelings about such matters as infidelity, so from a state of exalted happiness, I was plunged into despair.

Dion would not divulge who she was and I became obsessed with wondering why. Eventually, he confessed and told me a little about it. I visited her so I could see for myself what had attracted him. It ripped a big breach in my feeling for Dion. It was a turning point in our relationship. He was, of course, remorseful and tried to do things that would make me feel better about the matter.

Still, life must go on, and I continued to be creative and busy. We sold the Paint Pot to an art teacher and found a small store downtown in a great location. I called it "The Noir Gallery" and my products Noir Enamelcraft, after the black cat that I had so loved. I opened the gallery in October and sold almost everything I had when Christmas came around. I had to close the store in order to create a whole new stock to re-open.

Dion wanted to meet his real father. I suppose any child who had never met his biological parent has the urge to do this. We had a new car, a Ford pickup once again, but this time a brand new one. We drove all the way to Mexico City stopping along the way at quaint towns and villages. I particularly remember a place called San Blas where I collected a large stag beetle alive, but we had to kill it when it escaped its bamboo cage.

Upon reaching Mexico City, we set out to find Dion's famous father, Emelio Fernandez. He was noted for his bad attitude and gathered lots of notoriety for having killed a few people. Dion's mother had fallen in love with him in Hollywood where he was a stand-in for Valentino, but he had done something that caused Uncle Sam to deport him and had gone away without ever seeing Dion, never to return to the United States. Subsequently, he had made a name for himself in Mexico City and became not only an actor but one of their foremost directors. He had his own film studio, called "Azteca," for he believed he was of pure Aztec blood. His most famous film was *The Pearl*, a story by John Steinbeck.

Dion's father lived in a castle once owned by Cortez. I can remember arriving at the large iron gate that surrounded the edifice. The person who came to the door was a young lady. Dion told her he was the *hijo* (son) of Emelio Fernandez. She said he was not home and to come back later. This we did and eventually gained entrance.

Emelio was an imposing figure, but he clearly did not know how to handle the situation. He was torn between being kind to Dion and not wanting anyone to know he existed. The young woman we had met earlier had been the best friend of Emelio's daughter, Dion's half sister, but now she was Emelio's mistress. From what we could tell, this did not sit well with Emelio's daughter, who was nowhere to be seen.

We were invited to be guests at the fortress

and of course did not refuse. We spent a number of days with Emelio. Dion could speak films with him. Emelio took us to Tasco, showed us around Mexico City a little, and introduced us to a few film people. Then one night, back at the mansion, Emelio announced to Dion that he could kill him. We left the next morning without ever even saying goodbye.

This meeting seemed to have a profound effect on Dion. He may have acted as though it was just an adventure, but in reality I think he was deeply hurt by this rebuff. Never had his father helped him, even though he was entreated to do so by Dorothy. Now, when there was an opportunity to help Dion succeed in the film world, he would do nothing once again

We traveled back and resumed life in our Victorian house that was now quite a beauty. I had climbed a thirty-five foot scaffolding to paint it and had added gold leaf to its pilasters and fancy details. It was olive drab and black with gold touches. I had added special bottle glass windows and found a door that was being thrown out in a dumpster that exactly fitted our front door. It had a beveled oval window with beading around it and lots of carvings, so that it could be painted very decoratively.

The upstairs of the house was devoted to artwork and we had a photography dark room where Dion spent lots of time. I spent most of mine in the enameling room or the spacious painting studio which had plenty of wonderful north light.

For a time Dion worked at the Museum of Modern

Art in the Film Department, where his friend from childhood, Jerry Nordland, was the curator. But by then Dion had started to drink a lot and really was not up to the job, so it did not last long. This was another disappointment to me and I am certain to Dion.

Our beautiful ocelot died, probably because we did not know exactly how to feed him. We got two new ocelots with the intention of breeding them and dedicated a whole room in the back of our house to spend precious time with them, playing cat games.

Once we went to the Orient for a vacation, a healing trip for our stressed relationship. Dion scored some opium, which seemed to suit him well. He took enough back with him to use for a year. He was quite creative during this period as the opium satisfied his need.

Our time was our own and we could work when we wished, for we had no one to answer to but ourselves. We would also work on the house and the small garden, We had a saleswomen at The Noir Gallery, which was doing well. I would go there only on Saturdays where I could get in touch with my clientele. Our lives felt full and peaceful.

The "classic victorian" on Golden Gate Ave. 1965

Lora in the yard of the Victorian house with ocelot, 1968

Lancelot, Lora and Dion's first ocelot, 1966

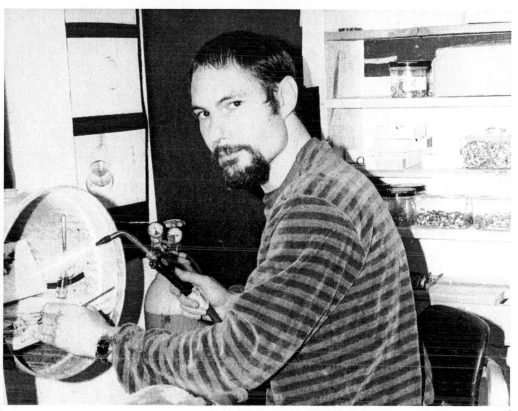

Dion soldering the enamel jewelry Lora made, 1968

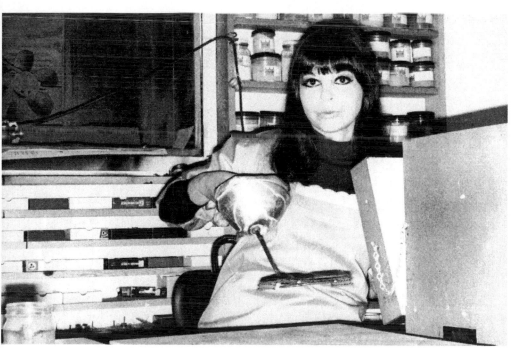

Lora at the enameling kiln that survived the fire, 1968

The Noir Gallery

*A*s life would have it, I had to move from the shop that Noir Gallery had done so well in because the building was to be torn down to make way for a big hotel. I searched for another location in the downtown area, but there wasn't much to choose from as it was beginning to be prohibitively expensive for small businesses. I did find a place on a side street a few steps off Market and Powell. Though it had not much walk-by traffic, I had a following and some customers found me, but it wasn't enough.

We had become acquainted with a young man who was in the jewelry business in Carmel. He did the gift shows in San Francisco and Los Angeles and invited us to share his booth. Noir

Enamelcraft did very well at these shows.

Again I had someone minding the store for me, only coming in on Saturdays to sell or sometimes in the evening to decorate the windows. Otherwise, I was at home furiously turning out the colorful enamelware that I became known for. Dion helped by soldering, but almost all the design work was mine. He spent much of his time in the dark room and working on his experimental films.

It was a pretty idyllic life. We seemed to have enough of everything. Our Victorian house was very special. It looked like a museum inside, with my butterfly and insect collection prominently displayed. We found a number of antiques that we added to our decor.

I remember getting an old spool cabinet from a big antique store down the street on Golden Gate Avenue. It was owned by a jovial black man and we had a conversation with him which culminated in a statement he made that I never forgot. It was simply two words: "Think Big."

It was about this period that we met Anton LeVey and his wife Diane. They appealed to our sense of the strange and unusual, as they had a full-grown lion living in their old Victorian house on California Street. We often went over to visit them late at night, for they preferred those hours. On Friday nights, Anton would give lectures on the occult and we would attend, along with a handful of others, listening to his collection of paranormal stories. Their home was painted black and contained many unusual objects, like a stuffed leopard that greeted you as you entered, a tombstone for a coffee table, and a host of books on all manner of esoteric subjects. On Sundays the four of us would go off on excursions together to visit people who were unconventional in some way. It was fascinatingly fun. Anton also had a movie projector and would show bizarre old movies late at night.

We got into the mysterious motif by purchasing an old hearse. For awhile we drove around in this strange automobile with purple velvet interior. It was also the time of the hippies and Haight Street wasn't far away. We went to a number of Love-Ins and of course the Fillmore Auditorium with its fabulous concerts.

Anton and Diane joined the Ocelot Club and we would go to meetings together. There were people from all walks of life who had big cats, not only ocelots. One day, Togare, their lion, ran rampant in the LeVey household, probably because they were boarding a pet leopard belonging to one of the San Francisco councilmen's son. After that they decided to give Togare to the San Francisco Zoo.

Anton was beginning to get a lot of notoriety, and some friends of his convinced him he should start a Satanist church. When he did, a lot of very peculiar people began to hang around his home. It was no longer very savory and Dion and I distanced ourselves. I had taken LSD a number of times, although for some reason Dion never did, which made me very sensitive to things that were happening. I somehow knew that when we no longer attended LeVey's gatherings, we would be ritually cursed. I realized I must deflect this psychic attack.

In looking back, I think that the curse turned into a blessing for me, but a true nightmare for Dion. His opium was gone and now there was no Cheracol to obtain, so he turned to drinking again. In addition, I am sure he must have been using heroin when he could obtain it. His behavior became bizarre and I began to be repulsed by him, which I never believed would be possible, as we were very connected.

However, the enamels were going well and I determined to get more help. It was difficult to do this as we were still working out of the Victorian house. I thought it would be better to have a workshop, and looked in the paper for such. The very first ad I called turned out to be the one. The realtor told me the two flats with workshop were on Isis Street, the only one-block long street in the entire city of San Francisco.

I had seen that street not long before when the LeVays and Dion and I were going on what we called an " investigative outing." I had announced, when seeing the street sign, that I would like to have a place on that street, and here it was. My interest in things Egyptian came into play, and I sensed that magic was also afoot. There was no question that this was to be where Noir Enamelcraft would be housed.

Dion's mother and stepfather rented the upstairs

flat and we worked on the two floors below. We set up the space and began producing in earnest, hiring help to accelerate our output.

After a time, Dion and I really started to have serious trouble in our relationship. I could not stand to be around his persona when he was on drugs or drinking and I could never know when this was going to occur. When I discovered one day that he had spent all our savings, which was about $10,000, I decided to end our marriage of twenty years.

We divided our properties by me getting the business and him keeping the Victorian house. I then needed the apartment that his parents occupied, to live in myself and had to ask them to leave. They did, but they did not speak to me anymore after that, even though I would continue to see Dion intermittently, for we never could stay apart from each other for long. He would attempt to clean up his act and call me and I would succumb to his winning ways when he was not under the influence of drugs.

I learned to drive and owned a lavender Corvette as well as a new van for the business. I also moved the gallery to a new location downtown, quite a large shop across from two theatres on Geary Street. It would be open at night for shoppers after the theaters let out.

About this time I noticed that I was having a physical problem, so I visited a doctor. It was discovered I had a tumor in my uterus and would have to have an operation that would negate my

ever having children. Dion and I had never wanted children and took care not to cause pregnancy.
Now I knew for certain I would never raise a family. The operation was a success and the tumor proved nonmalignant. I healed and went slowly back to work.

I can remember feeling very alone at that time. One morning as I was recuperating, a song came to me from nowhere and I recorded it on a tape. It was a song about Isis with a splendid melody and it went like this:

Isis is silver,
Isis is gold,
Isis is young,
Isis is old,
Isis is air,
Isis is mold,
Isis is timid,
Isis is bold,
All that Isis is, is as yet untold,
Isis is all that is, is what Isis is.

I was surprised at this channeling and wondered about it. Certainly I had noticed that being at Isis Street had produced some miraculous happenings.
I had moved my pair of ocelots there and they soon produced a cub I called Omar. This was very unusual because ocelots rarely breed in captivity, and to this day I still have success in breeding ocelots. Papyrus grew in the backyard, though I had not planted it. Other songs came.

Lots of synchronistic things occurred, as well. One day I found posters on Haight Street with just the word "IS" on them, so I purchased two of them and put them in my front window: ISIS. The Isis phenomenon was definitely beginning.

I went to a book store and was drawn to a book because of its color. It was titled *Isis*. I found a small volume of poetry by H.D. and opened it to a poem on Isis. The license plate on my lavender corvette was my address: 22ISIS. I learned that the number 22 was a magical number relating to the major arcana of the tarot.

I studied various occult subjects and one evening received a strange phone call from an anonymous person, who said she was a white witch. She advised me to read the works of Dion Fortune. The author's name of course intrigued me, so I found several books by her and continued for some time to read them at intervals. She was a noted English author connected to the Golden Dawn, but eventually she started her own group, The Servants of Light. Her books fascinated me. Dion Fortune has been a catalyst introducing the Goddess Isis into many lives.

Orders continued to come in fast and furiously for Noir Enamelcraft. One day, I was walking around the corner to mail some letters when the man who owned the factory building that adjoined the Isis Street property was coming out the door. I had often fantasized about obtaining that building, which formed a wall in my backyard. I could visualize cutting out the concrete in the back and putting in a glass door. I stopped him and on a whim asked him if he wanted to sell. Surprisingly, he told me he was going to be moving and we thereupon struck a deal for me to purchase that warehouse.

It was 2000 sq. feet and two stories with two bathrooms and a drive-in door. It seemed much bigger than I needed to enlarge my operations. I had a big party when I first got the keys and it was empty. It was a film party and we showed experimental work of the local filmmakers.

After that we got down in earnest to building the needed facilities to put this workshop together and make more enamelcraft than ever. Dion had once again surfaced to get involved and help me in this endeavor. He designed clever work stations with ways for the tiny colored granules to be exhausted from the air so that it would not get into the lungs of the workers. It wasn't long before forty employees were working away, making the huge line of colorful enamelcraft on all sorts of items that I designed.

Once, when Dion was again out of my life, I thought to take an art class in the area. It was a nostalgic feeling to sit down with a drawing board and sketch the figure before me. I did quite well, still having the touch, even though my art had for a long time consisted of making designs that I cut out of paper as stencils, much as I had always done with paper dolls as a little girl.

I met a man in this drawing class. We went out

afterward and he invited me to his apartment. I was intrigued by him, an accomplished artist who worked for an advertising firm. Perhaps it brought back memories of when I was a youth at art school, His girlfriend had just left him and it was inevitable that we should end up in bed, both of us alone and lonely, at the time. He was fifteen years my junior, but I had no intention of divulging my age. He was a very gentle lover. I was touched when he kissed the scar from my recent operation that I found so ugly, and delighted when he rolled out a gorgeous Persian rug so I might step upon it as I alighted from his bed.

He had other talents, like making beautiful stained glass lamps and collecting interesting artifacts for his home. I particularly recall a party put on by the wealthy patron who had purchased Dion's film. It was at a fancy hotel and I was wearing one of the interesting garments that I made. I still somehow found time to sew my own clothes, even though I must have been extremely busy. It was a slinky black dress with cuffs that matched the black feather boa that I wore with it.

Dion was there with Pat Marx, an avant guard film maker, who was now living at the Victorian house on Golden Gate Avenue, but it was just a platonic relationship, I am sure. However, I had heard that Dion was having an affair with Delores Baldwin, a relative of his friend Gerard. She had visited him from her home in L.A. where she was in the animation business. I also found out that she had also had a long term relationship with Frank, my old boyfriend from art school days. I could hardly believe such a coincidence could happen. It sometimes seems that there are things that are ordained and we are all in some way mysteriously connected.

Anyway, there we were each in the arms of another person, dancing at this party. It seemed very strange. Dion and I were not on good terms and I can not remember why, exactly, but I suppose it had something to do with his falling back into the world of drugs. Perhaps I had heard of his liaison with Delores and was disturbed by it, even though I should not have cared one iota.

The ocelots had bred once again. For a time, Dion kept one of the offspring but he had decided to sell the Victorian house, so I took the kitten to my backyard at Isis Street. Although it made me very sad, he did sell and bought another house with several apartments and had his parent move in. I suppose this allowed him to have some money that could sustain him and his habit.

I remember going back to our Victorian house one more time to see if there was anything of mine still left. The butterfly collection had been eaten by mites and all the wonders that I had created within this house seemed utterly destroyed. I once had so much hope for it to be a wonderful home for the two of us.

The ocelots proliferated in the backyard of Isis Street and the space was getting a little crowded. There was a garden adjoining and I began to covet it.

One day, I talked to the people over the back fence and they told me they were moving to Seattle to retire, so I made a deal to purchase their home, It was a rather ugly Victorian with two apartments, facing Folsom Street, but the yard was a nice addition. I built more cages there to house the beautiful spotted cats I loved.

Now I had three buildings that joined together in the back yard, one painted yellow, one orange, and the new one was to be painted three shades of purple with black pillars and touches of gold.

The house needed lots of work. I decided to make it as interesting as I could. Although it was a relatively simple Victorian, I believed it could be enhanced by adding gingerbread. There was a little window with a porch way up high, but no access to this unless I tore the ceiling out, which I did. In fact, I ended up tearing out the walls of three rooms until there was one very large room. It took a long time to create the space exactly as I imagined it, but finally it was complete.

Dion moved in with me for awhile, only to be asked to leave once again. I have never chronicled the comings and goings of our relationship, so filled with turmoil and disappointment, as they were.

I added stained glass to my artistic repertoire by taking classes so I could design and make windows for my new house. I designed three windows of Egyptian motif to be installed in the three front windows.

I also added some colorful glass hangings to my line of enamelcraft. There was a stairway in the

Noir Gallery leading to a small space that I set up with lights that would show off the glass windows I designed. It was quite magical down there and I got a unique idea. I called it the psychic underground and had lecturers come in from time to time to impart their wisdom to those interested. It also helped to promote the stained glass.

The house on Folsom Street was photographed a lot and appeared in the book *Painted Ladies*, a collection of colorfully painted houses in the city. Although not a classic Victorian like the one on Golden Gate Avenue, it was enhanced on the outside by carvings that Dion had cleverly made for the sides of each window. I had added a huge enamel mural with an outer space design to its facade. I would get notes from people who enjoyed the fact that I had cared to put the house together in this way, a delight for their eyes as they walked down this not-too-colorful street.

The interior was also unique. I created a bridge to tie the structure together so the huge expanse could exist. I got a white rug for it, which I sprayed with rainbow colors making it a rainbow bridge. One could go from a large sleeping loft to another loft to the small window that started me off doing this in the first place. I enhanced the window by adding a decorative fireplace carving that fitted around it, giving it small columns and a ledge where I placed a Buddha statue - soon to be replaced by a Goddess statue. It was a place of meditation.

I decorated the tall pillar that held up the
bridge in the living room with enamel tiles depicting
hieroglyphs designating the four directions and
rubrics from the ancient *Egyptian Book of the Dead*. The
stained glass windows I designed and installed had
Egyptian motifs of the Eye of Horus, the Solar Disk
and an ankh, all fitted with crystals and set in a lotus
and rainbow design. On a bright sunny day, rainbows
played on the walls in a magical way. I called it "the
rainbow time."

The downstairs included my office, the kitchen
and dining room, with large glass doors that looked
out on the garden full of ocelots. It was a wonderful
place for them, as it was closed on all sides and
I could let the ocelots out in the garden without
fear of having them run off. Before I knew it, I had
six, and because I now lived in the purple house, I
engaged someone to live in the top of the Isis Street
house to help care for them.

Noir Enamelcaft was thriving, and I needed to
keep all forty employees happy so I created a way
for them to have a four day week, working ten hours
a day, except when the orders got too big and then
there was overtime. I was very engrossed in the
production of the enamelware, designing constantly
new motifs and new objects on which to apply them.

I was active in the Ocelot Club and put on a
convention for them in San Francisco. It was quite
successful and well attended. However, during that
very time a lot of notoriety happened around a

family who had kept a mountain lion tied up in their backyard and ended up having a little girl mauled by the big cat. Some people who did not know how to take care of their animals ruined it for the rest of us in California, for soon after this incident laws began to be created stipulating that no exotic animals would be allowed within the confines of San Francisco.

I had, at the time, six ocelots, three bush babies and a tarantula. It was a situation that was difficult to cope with and I can recall attending several hearings with supervisors and trying my best to overturn this ruling. I was given the okay to have the cats I had, but would not be allowed to continue to breed them— and I would have a host of inspections from many sources if I chose to keep ocelots in San Francisco.

I became discouraged and decided to look in the paper for country properties. Under this heading I found a very intriguing ad and determined to go see it. The ad stated that there was a turn of the century farmhouse, a church, a commercial kitchen, and a twenty-two room lodge to be had in the wine country of Sonoma County. At the time I was reading Dion Fortune's *Moon Magic*, and its heroine, Morgan Le Fay, finds a church building which she makes into her home. She performs rituals to Isis within it.

I was fascinated with the idea of a church and set up a day to go and check that property out. I took some friends with me, Ed Taylor, who had helped me survive the fire, and Clifford Ghames, my caretaker for the animals who lived upstairs on Isis Street.

We arrived at the place, seventy-five miles north
of San Francisco, in the small town of Geyserville.
The grass of its 8.5 acres had not been mowed and
was very tall, almost over my head. There was a large
commercial kitchen all right, but the dining room
had been torn down, leaving only a concrete slab in
its wake. The lodge contained only twelve rooms
with large bathrooms on the first floor and plans for
building other rooms upstairs in the one enormous
room that measured 30x80 feet. The upstairs had
windows all around and more bathrooms. It was very
run down, but I could imagine fixing it up.

The church, with its redwood walls and rows
of windows, had a small stage and a high beamed
ceiling and hardwood floor. The "swimming pool"
was just a muddy hole.

The farmhouse was situated under the shade
of a 500-year -old Douglas fir tree. We knocked
on the door after our so far self-guided tour. A
German woman answered. She told me she had
been married to the owner but he had become a
woman. She proceeded to show me clippings from
a newspaper about him/her. She said if I was really
interested in the property, I should try to purchase
it from this person who had a restaurant in San
Francisco. I inquired as to which one and was told
it was the Castle Grand.

Now that was just too much of a coincidence, as
that restaurant was right across the street from my
purple house on Folsom Street, and I had dined there

often. Chills played along my spine when I heard this revelation and I was determined to meet this person. So, upon my return, I did.

Alexis was there. She was a very attractive 6'2" woman with red hair and a nervous demeanor. She kept shaking the bangles on her many bracelets as she spoke. I told her I had been out to see her property in Geyserville and that I might be interested if she could lower the asking price. She said she'd give it some thought.

Some time went by while I mused about that unique property now and then. One day Alexis phoned me and made me an offer. She was willing to sell to me for $100,000 less than the asking price. I said I would need to see the place again and sleep overnight there before making up my mind. She agreed, and I took some friends, Dr. Weinesland and Clifford, along with a pet ocelot, to spend Hallowe'en night at the Lodge in Geyserville.

It was a strange and eerie night. Those that lived on the property were not very cordial. I assumed they did not wish to leave this wonderful place. The lounge in the lodge had a rug with two footsteps mysteriously burned into it. We made a fire in the fireplace and sat around it in the dark, for there was no electricity. The next morning we found a dead chicken in the grasses of the overgrown lawn,

There was an earthy woman and her young girl child living behind the theatre, the only one who seemed somewhat friendly. She told me about the history of the place.

The land had been under the auspices of the Baha'i for seventy years as a summer school. Baha'i is a faith that studies all the religious philosophies of the world and believe their leader, Baha'u'llah, was a prophet from God along with all the other prophets from each religion. A man called John Bosch, a wine master, had lived in the main house on the premises, but when traveling on a train he met a women who introduced him to this new faith, so he gave up his profession. The Baha'i did not believe in drinking wine. Bosch sent for a Baha'i bride, mail order. Her name was Louise, and together they devoted themselves to the task of creating a Baha'i school. When they died, since they had no children, they gave the land to the Baha'i who vacated it when the 101 freeway cut through through their land.

What was left was the eight and a half acres. Alexis, then Alex, was the highest bidder when the State of California auctioned off the land. He was tall and redheaded, wore a black cape and looked very strange. The townsfolk at the auction were quite concerned about who it was that was getting the property, but none of them bid higher.

During the time Alex was there, he had the operation transforming him into a woman. Alexis lost interest in the land and rented it to Dennis Perone. The others who were living on the property were involved with Dennis, who operated a marijuana store in San Francisco. He had gotten notoriety when he accosted a policeman at his store and was now mostly in San Francisco dealing with his legal problems. It was he who put the ad in the paper about the sale of the property, and he to whom I first spoke on the phone. He was leasing it from Alexis in hopes of making it into a kind of gay hippie haven, but had realized that in no way would he ever be granted the ability to do this from the planning committee of Sonoma County, as the townfolk wanted them out.

Geyserville was not a redneck town, but was full of wineries and people involved in the wine industry for the most part. Drugs and homosexuality were not acceptable to them and they were ever-watchful as the property was up for sale for some time. The Russian River was just a few blocks away and the place had potential as a bed and breakfast because of the wineries that folks liked to visit.

I was strictly looking into how it might fit into my business. There would be plenty of room for the animals, that much was certain. I wondered how I might be able to manage to move everything here and if I could carry on with the downtown gallery and train a bunch of new people to do the glass and enamel work I was now turning out in large quantities.

I went off to be with my sister and her husband and their children for a vacation in Vail, Colorado. It was quite an experience to be in the snow, the whiteness surrounding me while I thought of my options. Caryl's husband was an economist and when I told him about the deal he encouraged me to make the investment. I was feeling very adventurous then and was open to something new. I went back home determined to follow through. I called Alexis and we proceeded with the deal.

During that time, Dion was to be released from a halfway house where he'd been trying once again to kick his insidious habit. He called and assured me he was doing well and would never use drugs again. My obtaining possession of the property and his getting out of this treatment center coincided, and I asked him to be a caretaker there, thinking that it would be good for him to be in the country, away from the temptations waiting in the city.

Geyserville was a small town of only 1500 people most of them residing in the pastoral hills around the valley. There were small wineries everywhere and the landscape was dotted with vines.

It was called Geyserville because the town was situated beneath Geyser Peak, a smooth high mountain wherein powerful geysers gushed mysteriously before the PG&E tapped into it for energy. Still steamy clouds rose out of this peak, on some days, painting the sky with white striations that added to the picturesque beauty of the landscape.

Best of all, there was a river that ran through the town that I did not know about when I first bought the property. It could be reached by walking through an orchard. I remember finding it for the first time and delightedly studying the many colors of the wet river stones in the sparkling water. Here you could watch white crane and great blue heron go fishing for their morning breakfast.

There was a bridge over the river where you could walk or bicycle to the Grange Hall where townsfolk gathered once a month for a delicious dinner complete with wine from one of the many wineries in the area. It was a town with a history, being larger than Los Angeles in the 1850's, I found out, which was quite a surprise since it was only one block long with a handful of businesses. There was a blacksmith shop, a grocer, an antique store and gift shop, an old fashioned diner, complete with pool table and a famous Italian Restaurant where people came from afar to dine on copious dinners. The hardware store was just as it had been around the turn of the century and everyone knew everyone else.

I imagined that this would be a perfect environment for Dion who might heal in these surroundings. I envisioned him leaving the drug world behind, getting inspired by the beauty of the land, so that once again, he might use his wonderful talents as an artist and filmmaker.

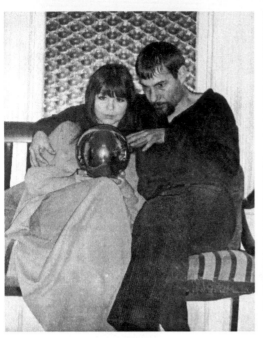

Lora and Dion trying to see into the future, 1969

*Lora and Dion wearing third eye
and reading Isis Unveiled*

Lora in the first Noir Gallery at Sutter and Stockton, 1968

The Isis Street workshop and two flats with ISIS sign, 1970

The purple house on Folsom Street, 1971

ISIS OASIS *is* BORN

*I*n any case, I would need to have someone to oversee things at the property, as I was planning to hire people to fix everything up. I still had a factory and my shop to run in San Francisco and there was so much to do in both places. Dion readily agreed to take on the assignment and I also arranged for my cousin Curtis to be there. I found some other guys to build cages and certain things that were imperative.

Almost everything in the old farmhouse was as originally built. All of the walls and ceilings were made with thin slats of redwood that had been varnished but thankfully never painted. The windows were made of little panes of glass with built in screens that pulled down. There was, in addition to the living room and kitchen, a dining room and a study on the first floor.

The staircase was most spectacularly lovely, going up to a landing with a little porch and window in the door that looked out on Geyser Peak. There were three bedrooms and a sun porch all in a row and you had to go through one room to get to the others. What had probably been the master bedroom at one time had been turned into a bathroom with three sinks and three toilets in stalls. There was no shower or bathtub, but I found them later in a barn behind the house that must have been the outhouse. This would have to change.

Dion stayed in the study downstairs on a mat on the floor and when I came, I stayed upstairs. Curtis stayed in the Lodge. Every weekend I tried to bring up a truckload of furniture to outfit the old farmhouse. One of the first pieces was a large sideboard with a thick marble top. It was made of a rosewood that matched the walls of the house.

The rest of the property was still occupied by some of the previous tenants, a fellow called Faglebee and others, who continued to stay on and seemed loath to leave. Once when I was asleep in the loft of my purple house, where I retreated each night to my fake-fur covered bed, I received a call from Curtis. He was quite excited and told me that he had found a patch of marijuana growing beside the pond surrounded by trees. He was going to call the sheriff. I calmed him down and told him instead to threaten the folks that were hanging on, but give them the option to harvest their crop and leave. This worked like a charm and the next time I drove up they were gone.

There were so many repairs to do I could not even imagine how to begin. Then, by some miracle, some German fellows magically arrived to help in the work. This was a Goddess-send. One was a charming young man named Ulle. I had set up the upstairs of the Lodge as a stained glass studio and was planning to do that as well as my enamel work up there. I wanted to add lots of stained glass to the property. I hired a Cuban fellow to help with the stained glass, who was also a filmmaker and an intellectual. He and Dion hit it off right away.

I found a plumber to dismantle the bathroom in the old house and redo it. I brought an old-fashioned bathtub from Isis Street, the kind with the beast feet, and it was placed on a platform in the middle of the room. A very old-fashioned toilet was given to me by a friend. It had a round tank and a push button and was quite unique.

Also, I purchased from my old friend, who used to own the Bagel Shop and had gone into the antique business, a fabulous long counter made in France. It contained three sinks and a multitude of drawers. It tilted to let the water out and you needed a foot pedal to turn the water on. It spanned one whole wall of the enormous bathroom.

There were many peacocks that lived on

the property and they were wild and noisy. One neighbor had complained about them and the animal regulation department sent a letter saying they had to go. I called the veterinary school at the university at Davis and asked them if they could de-voice the males. They said no problem. So, it was Dion's chore to catch them and build a large cage to transport them. He actually managed to catch them and drive them to Davis for the operation that would remove their voices. He also installed new linoleum in the kitchen of the old house.

He was doing pretty well, it seemed, and I was hopeful of his recovery. I remember one night I let him come into my bedroom and we made love again. It seemed so sad to me that there had ever been the heroin horror in our lives that caused such pain and severed our relationship that had been so full of vitality.

I returned to the city as usual to continue my enamel work and the multitude of things I was involved in there. Dion had an appointment to see a dentist in San Francisco. Two of his teeth had become loose and had to be removed. He was quite depressed about this. From a very handsome man, he had deteriorated a great deal. He had bags under his eyes, his skin had become coarse, and his hair scraggly and long. He wore a beard but he did not keep it looking trim. He hadn't lost his innate intelligence, though, and his ability to do so many diverse things. I felt very sorry for him.

He came to see me at the purple house and told

me for the first time ever that he needed some money for heroin, for he could not go through the dentist routine without first fortifying himself in this way. He asked me for $50 for this purpose and I could not refuse.

On that day, I was downtown at the Noir Gallery when Tony, my factory manager called. He said that Dion was at the hospital. I hastily made my way to where Dion lay in the corridor with only his feet sticking out from the gurney. I was told that he was most likely brain dead because he had been unconscious a long time prior to when they received him. He had been brought to the hospital by a black man and the orange truck he had been driving was in the parking lot.

I knew that it was the end. I signed the papers allowing them to try to save his life and left, never to return. He lay in a coma for seven days. It was an overdose of heroin. I never expected this horrible outcome.

I was in a shocked state for awhile. I can remember lying on the sofa in the living room of my purple house, with the rays of rainbows touching me from the prismatic stained glass windows, soothing me, at last, to sleep. When I awoke, I called the hospital to find out that no change had taken place. I talked to Dorothy, Dion's mother, on the phone for the first time since our estrangement from the divorce five years earlier, but I do not remember the exact words. What could we have said? I turned the whole fiasco over to her, for I simply could not face being involved.

I decided to go back to the country, to the place I now called Isis Oasis. Here I could gain solace from the huge old tree and be in the greenery that was beginning to be so important to me. I was playing harp music by Georgia Kelly, called *Seapeace*, all the way up Highway 101 and to this day I think of this time when I play that music, it's so haunting.

As I approached Geyserville, I drank in the beautiful scenery that would always stimulate and astound me. The hills hold such a wonderful light and there is so much delicacy between the spaces of the trees and the vines, row upon row. I thought of Dion and how he suffered and perhaps could never really take in the special quality of this land in his state of mind.

As I drove into the driveway of the antique farmhouse, my new home in the country, a strange thing happened. I stopped the van, opened the front door of the house and went back to fetch my bags. Then I saw it. A fantastic looking large and colorfully decorated snake basking in the sun on the path. I went to find my caretaker, old Ned, who was tending the garden on the next level. I asked if he would come down and see the snake and make sure it was not poisonous and also help me in with my things.

When we got back to the van, the snake had vanished. Ned carried the bags in and I thanked him and then told him of the situation with Dion and that I had come to spend some quiet time during this interval that I suspected would end in his death. Ned, who always reminded me of an ancient Egyptian mummy, nodded gravely and left.

I was standing there in the middle of the room, a bit bewildered and forlorn when suddenly I saw in the corner, wrapped around a small marble altar table, the snake that had met me on the path. My heart stood still as I watched it twisting around the beast feet of the table, which held a large print of Osiris, ancient Egyptian God of the Underworld. I wondered how such a thing could happen.

Still, not knowing what sort of snake it was, I bolted from the house to find Ned again and tell him that the snake had come inside. He returned and with the aid of a long-handled broom coaxed the snake from the corner and out the door, where it slithered down the stairs and disappeared.

To this day I have never seen such a snake on the property, let alone inside the house. The thought struck me that the dead or dying might have the power to return in the form of an animal and that perhaps that was Dion's way of saying goodbye.

Then, three crystal doorknobs came off in my hand as I opened three different doors. This had an ominous effect on my psyche.

An old friend of Dion's came by and several other people, to console me, so that I was not alone, but I did find some time for mourning in the old house with its dark wood walls. I wrote a bit about my feelings. Even though we both experienced other lovers in our lives, our bond was very powerful and I had always dreamed that Dion would recover from drugs and that we would be together again. I can recall the feeling of being in the living room of the old house that I was just starting to move into. I wrote in my diary:

My room is my tomb
Things about me that I revere
Statue of a cat...peacock feathers...books
Colors come with it, woven into a fanciful tapestry
I would like you permanently here, as I always wished you to be.
But you have finally eluded my space
Your presence never again to be here.

The days wore on and Dion continued to lie lifeless in the hospital. His mother refused to believe he was, for all practical purposes dead. On July 2nd, the sixth day of the coma I wrote the following:

Where are you now . . . can you see what's happening?
I tried to give you beauty and life here on Earth and you
ignored my offering
Preferring instead the needle and the booze.
I have known sorrow and grief beyond belief
But I can handle tomorrow anyhow somehow.
I knew I'd have to face the future alone
It seems as though I'd had time to prepare

This place in which I'd had such wonderful visions for us
A togetherness such as we'd never known before could never
have been.
You'd have turned it into a bad dream anyway
You liked nightmares and somnambulism
While I flourished on daydreams and delights
Our paths long ago had taken different turns
There is no turning back upon the way
You will go into the darkness...the unknown.
I loved you still even though you'd turned your back on my desires
and cared for me only so far as you could use me.
And I let you...rather than losing you entirely
I figured I lost you longer ago than just a little while
I have heard you had a secret soul mate
to whom you must have turned in your pain
And since there was no changing you
No point in rearranging the events that lead up to your eventuality
What is left is for me to put in place all things.
To find another life, another love
To fill my final days with pleasure...would be what I would wish.
A partner such as I have never known to be my own.
A close and gentle relationship.
You freed me for this...as I could not do it with you still present
Upon the Earth.
No one could possibly take your place while you were here.
I kept on waiting for the end of your addiction
Lost in a comatose state
Between eternity and nothingness
Getting what you deserved
I knew it all along

There was no escape.
You had your drugs in spite of everything
A deaf ear turned to those who pleaded otherwise
And now there is no more anything.
We said goodbye to our love long ago...
But I could not believe such a passing of our story could occur
And lingered longer than I needed, fearing always to give
you up totally.
You slipped from my grip as I tried to keep your sanity alive.
You ruthlessly tried to destroy all I kept building
Still I was so unwise as to keep you close to me
Fearing always to be entirely without you.
Now I am face to face with losing you
Forever now...there is no choice
Unless you come around
Resurrected as before in the myth of Isis and Osiris.

Some of the people that came to see me did a ceremony at
midnight on the 3rd of July in the old church to resurrect
your body. May you find yourself in a place that you wish to be.
Tomorrow we will see where that will be.

Yes, the 4th of July was the end. Dorothy
decided to have them pull the plug. I could hear the
fireworks going off around me. Dion had loved the
4th and we would always go to the fireworks together.
And so, on this day I began my journey alone.

I returned to the studio in the city and continued
to run the factory and the gallery as before. One day,
when I felt stronger, I opened the closet that Dion

had used on the second floor of the design studio on Isis Street. He had an ingenious method for locking and opening the door by touching a nail in the floor. It was where I thought he was storing his film equipment, When I looked inside I found only an enormous jumble of bloody cottons and deflated colored balloons.

There were still some things he had not pawned: his left-handed bow (a Sagittarius, he loved archery) and his Ariflex camera and tripod and a few miscellaneous things. In a very short time all of these found their way into the hands of others who needed them, even a left-handed archer. Perhaps Dion had wished to distribute them in some way to those who would make the best use of them.

I remember wishing I could show the bloody syringes to his mother so she might see the evidence of the endless waste I witnessed. Of course, she knew he was a heroin addict, but how much did she really understood about what addiction meant: the destruction of a talented human being. A lot of the love I had for Dion was for his talent. His mother loved him as only a mother could love a son, completely and without reservations.

I had to gather my strength together to carry on with the huge task of maintaining my factory, gallery, and country property, as well as the animals in my care. How I could do this is nothing short of a miracle, and I began to believe that the Goddess was helping me in some plan that only she knew. I was simply a vehicle for her will.

Many things came my way in great profusion. I would sometimes close my eyes and visualize all that I had been given and it seemed that there was a vast abundance thrown at me at this time. Miracles came my way that were untold. People came into my life that gave me the impetus to carry on with this dream of creating something of significance.

In spite of the overwhelming tasks that I took on, I persisted in believing that the Goddess was behind every activity I was propelled to accomplish. I could not possibly have been able to do so much without her help. It was a time of total amazement for events materialized one after the other. It seemed I was utilizing abilities that I did not know I had.

I began to believe that there was a spirit in the antique house I inhabited on the land that wanted me to bring forth a new concept. This spirit disclosed to me that something was missing from the many religions the Baha'i had studied previously on this land: the Goddess! I believed that I was here to bring the divine feminine to the forefront on this sacred land and to eventually be a catalyst to expand this idea. I began to see clearly the rationale for creating change, in order to balance this lopsided mixed-up world.

I felt guided here for this divine purpose yet at this point was unclear as to how I might accomplish such a shift in the minds of the masses.

Stained glass doors of Isis and Osiris by Lora

Lora in the Lodge lounge with her cat, Macho, 1978

The 500-year-old Douglas fir at Isis Oasis, 1978

Lora outside the old farm house at Isis Oasis, 1978

ISIS OASIS EVOLVES

After this tragedy, everything seemed like a jumble. The peacocks that Dion had captured and taken to be de-voiced all died, one by one, and I felt very sad. The vet school said the operation would be safe, but it was not.

I worked very hard, as has always been my way. I use work as a way to lose myself. It helps to keep me strong instead of feeling sorry for myself. I entered gift shows that generated the sales that kept the factory going. My booth was always attractive, filled with bright fanciful enamel designs. The stained glass line I designed were hanging pieces fitted with crystals that captured the eye of the buyers. Things were still going very well in the business and orders came in with great profusion.

As for Isis Oasis, I had hired a caretaking couple who lived in one of the rooms of the Lodge. The county had given me a list to accomplish in order to operate as a business, on which they inserted the words "financially unfeasible." The property had changed from commercial status to rural residential during escrow, which no one had told me.

Still, I persisted and tried to make myself known to the community. I designed a float for them which won an award in a parade in the little town of Healdsburg, not far from Geyserville, and so the town folks realized that they had nothing to fear. A local writer did a piece on me in the *Healdsburg Tribune*, and that also helped.

I outfitted the theatre with chairs I had purchased from my friend's antique shop in San Francisco and put on an opera. Not many people showed up, but it was great fun to do it. There were professional singers from the San Francisco Opera Company presenting excerpts from *Madame Butterfly,* and it was inspiring to take part in it. I imagined other presentations utilizing the theatre.

I wanted to start a nonprofit organization, something Dion and I had spoken of. I knew I needed a lawyer and one day when I was simply going through some papers I came across a paper advertising shell lamps on which a card was stapled. The card was that of Roberta Cook, attorney at law. The lamp company was in Los Angeles on Isis Street. I thought this very strange, and upon detaching the card, I found handwritten on the back the words "I am interested in Isis."

My cousin, Curtis, had given me the card. He had
a gift shop where he sold Noir Enamelcraft. Roberta
had bought some enamels and given Curtis her card. He
had stapled it onto a larger sheet of paper he had lying
around, knowing that I might lose something small.

It was just a coincidence that the lamp company's
address was on Isis Street. Or was it? This is one of
the strange phenomena that happen on a regular basis
to me, as it does when one taps into the Goddess
Isis, as I was beginning to do.

The strange coincidence prompted me to phone
this lawyer, Roberta Cook. She listened to my story
and decided to come out to meet me at Isis Oasis.
Thus began our long lasting friendship. Roberta
helped me get the Isis Society for Inspirational
Studies started. Its purpose was to bridge the gap
between ancient Egypt and the new age.

After awhile the German fellows had to go back
to Germany and I was seeking some new help to work
at Isis Oasis. I ran an ad in the *San Francisco Chronicle*
and lots of guys showed up to interview at my factory
in the city. One of them was William Mitchell.

William was tall and good-looking and about
my age, but did not seem the type to be considering
a caretaking position, and I did not hire him. He
told me he was interested in being in the country
and asked if he could come out to see the property
anyway. He showed up one weekend and I took him
around. He gave me lots of suggestions and we

shared a little about our lives. Back in the city, he called me and invited me to dinner and a movie. That is how our romance began.

The movie starred Paloma Picasso and I was amazed when William told me he had been like a father to her. He had been Françoise Gillot's lover after she left Pablo Picasso and had lived with her for seven years in Paris. He had been brought up in New York City and met his French wife at Columbia University. He had gone to France with her and fathered two children. Their relationship ended, then he met Françoise.

After fifteen years in France, William returned to the U.S.A. and worked in the stock market and as a voice-over actor. He had a beautiful voice, very melodious and with perfect diction. He was also a poet and songwriter. While in New York he was duped out of all his savings, so he went to L.A. to try his hand at acting, but with no success.

He was living in an apartment not far from Isis Street. He did not have too much to fall back on and I offered him a position helping around the factory. We began to spend more time together.

One Saturday I was in my gallery when my old friend, Ed Taylor, dropped in. We went out to coffee and I picked up the local advertiser, announcing I was going to find something interesting therein. Checking the furniture ads, I spied one that started with "Egyptian Furniture." It was obviously a must that I call that number.

This is how I met Val Noble (later Coro, but

she has changed her name a number of times.) She lived not far from my abode in the city, so I went to see what she had and purchased a number of things for the country house. Her way was to decorate in motifs and she was tired of Egyptian and wanted to do Japanese next. She liked second hand stores and taught me to shop in them. She was always free in the afternoon as she lived on government money declaring herself to be incompetent to work. It was enough to live on and she could do a little acting on the side, as that was her passion.

She was putting on a one-woman play at Project Artaud, which I attended. William was my escort. I invited a number of friends to the show and then to my house for the evening. I called it a "purple party" and wrote the invitations using all P's on purple paper. After dancing romantically with me and singing in my ear with his lovely voice, William ended up in my bed. It was the first night that he did not go home. After awhile, he took up residence with me and helped me greatly to overcome the many steps that I needed to complete for the county ordinances and to jump start the Isis Society for Inspirational Studies.

By now all the cats were at Isis Oasis and Clifford had moved out of the upstairs of Isis Street and was replaced by my nieces, who were to assist with my house by cleaning and caring for it. The bush babies still lived downstairs in the design studio, as we had not yet built a cage for them at Isis Oasis.

Each weekend we would go to the country and

work there, then return to do work in the city. William accompanied me to L.A. for the gift show in January and at the one in S.F. as well. It felt good to have a companion again and he did try to work with me on what was important to accomplish.

My friend Judy Smith was engaged to be married and wanted her wedding at Isis Oasis. She was quite a wild woman, given to drinking too much. She was marrying an accountant, by the name of Del Pelzel. She asked me to perform the wedding, since I had gotten a minister's license from the Temple of Man when I visited Bob Alexander while at the Los Angeles gift show.

Bob Alexander was an old friend who had begun the church in Venice, California. It was devoted to the arts and those who belonged were all artists. When members passed away, he would commemorate them with plaques in his garden. Wally Berman, an avant garde artist, had died in an accident and was among the first to attain the honor. Many more have followed.

In any case, I agreed to officiate at the wedding, which was to have an Egyptian theme. William did not like Judy and did not want me to hold the wedding at Isis Oasis. It was our first rift, but I went ahead and arranged it anyway. Judy planned to have belly dancers, musicians and costumes of ancient Egypt. This appealed to me. I studied up on Egyptian ritual in order to create a ceremony that would be somewhat authentic.

When the time came, William did not want to be

there. He was to be doing some tests that week at a hospital since one day while dining (across the street at The Castle Grand!) he started to choke. One of the waiters, using the proper techniques, helped him recover, but William went to have this looked into.

I went off to perform the wedding and Coro came with me. It was a very lively wedding with many of Judy's friends attending, Most of them were habitués of North Beach bars. Although the wedding ceremony went well and I am certain looked beautiful to those attending, the event ended with a lot of drunkenness and disorder. I thought perhaps William was right after all. When it was over, Isis Oasis looked a mess. It was going to take a lot of work to put everything back in order.

I returned to the city and remember well the moment that William announced the verdict of the tests. He told me he had only two years to live. He had cancer of the esophagus,

I was aghast. He had told me that there was longevity in his family and he was expecting to live to a ripe old age, and now this. William forgave me my wedding decision and continued to assist me in many ways.

In the early stages, it was easier to adjust to the situation because he was still very healthy-looking. It didn't seem real. But it was. As time progressed, he began to change. He got disturbed at my nieces since they never seemed to have time to live up to their bargain of keeping the house clean. He gave them a talking to which resulted in their leaving. They were going to do so anyway, but I felt a little chagrined. William hired instead a young couple who proved to be a disaster. One of my star decorators took over the apartment thereafter.

The bush babies were moved to the upstairs of the lodge but they didn't do well there and eventually died without producing any offspring. The ocelots, however, did very well and began producing cubs. One of them went to a young girl in Cloverdale, the next town after Geyserville. She was a trombonist and played in a brass band. She wanted to bring her band to Isis Oasis for a concert. John, the young artist that I knew, had gotten in touch with me again and I invited him to come for a visit and enjoy the concert. He arrived by bus at midnight and William and I went to meet him. It was quite a humorous moment for as John stepped off the bus, William and he silently got into a mock battle *a lá High Noon*. They hit if off quite well after that.

The brass band came to Isis Oasis to play a free concert and there were more of them than people in the audience. I felt like royalty having this amazing band play just for us. Those shiny brass instruments against the now carefully manicured green lawn were quite a sight.

After I found out about William's condition, I began to look into the tenuousness of life. William and I decided to take a vacation in Europe. He wanted to go back there and see some old friends and even his wife and children. We made plans to leave. I had a silver Jaguar at the time and just before leaving we discovered that it had been stolen by a young guy who we had engaged to work on the roofs at Isis Oasis while we were gone. He had broken into my house and taken various objects along with the Jaguar. But we had our tickets and could not stay just because of that, so we went on to New York, our destination for a number of days.

William took me around to his haunts and we visited my New York sales rep, who invited us to his home for dinner. We toured the Metropolitan Art Museum and saw the Egyptian display there. I was enthralled with the temple that was built into one gallery. We walked around Greenwich Village. It must have been quite nostalgic for William. who had grown up in the Big City.

Finally we heard from my manager, Tony, that the Jaguar had been found along the freeway south of San Francisco. The car, typical of Jaguars, had stalled on the freeway and the guy stealing it had fled. Tony handled it for me and had it brought back to Isis Oasis.

Then we arrived in France. William had a good friend there who suggested a *pension* right next door to his dwelling. It was *trés* French. William was starting to lose a lot of weight and his clothes were hanging on him. Still, he had energy to visit his old friends with me. He went to see his ex-wife by himself, however, and I never got to meet her. His sons were elsewhere and he never got to see them. I went shopping by myself in the streets of Paris, coming home with a wonderful turquoise artist's smock. We rented a car and went off to the countryside where William had also lived and knew people. We visited many churches, castles, and, of course, excellent restaurants.

England was our next destination and we stayed at a brick b&b and went to a few plays, the British Museum with their great Egyptian collection, and visited more of William's old friends, the last time he would see them.

I remember reviewing in my mind a radio show that I had listened to, when I was very young, about just such a journey. Now I felt like one of the characters in this memorable radio play.

Upon returning home to my factory, I found in a stack of mail on my desk a notice from a labor union. It seems that my employees, in my absence, had been won over by a union and were attempting to unionize. I could not fathom this, as they had never complained to me about anything. The demands of the union would negate any funds that I could possibly make without raising prices drastically, and I could not go along with it. I decided to keep it at bay until we finished the Christmas orders we had. I had to get a very expensive labor lawyer. I decided to sell the business and put the word out.

Many people had an interest, but everything fell through until, strangely, a competitor decided he wanted it. He had already copied many of my designs and even sent spies to work for me. Maybe it was one of the spies that started the idea of the labor union. I know that the spokesman for the workers turned out to be a women who had become a close friend of my niece Jamie, who had lived in the Isis Street apartment and had worked as my secretary for a time. I learned that my niece was a lesbian and so was this employee who made an attempt to unionize. My niece, who had become her friend, could not make her back out.

I got all the orders done and then I sold my business to Juicy Productions, with a huge order from the Smithsonian and much good will. He paid me something down and Roberta handled the sale.

It was a trying time. I had to give in to what was happening, knowing it wasn't going to be easy.

One day when I was in the city I got a call from the caretakers at Isis Oasis. They told me that William had died. He had gone outside, stark naked and passed out under the ancient tree. An ambulance came for him and he did not go quietly into that dark goodnight, but instead cursed death as he died in the ambulance on the way to the hospital.

I came back from the city to pick up his ashes at the mortuary. I had a service for him with some of our local friends and planted a tree over the ashes as he had wished, a golden cyprus. I made a plaque for him with the words "he quested" which he had asked for. Today the tree has grown very tall and I can visit it at any time, touching its branches and sometimes I ask it questions and listen to what William might have to say.

So I was left alone again. William had been with me through the process of getting Isis Oasis started as a bed and breakfast with the hopes of it someday being a retreat center. He had been through the process of starting the Isis Society for Inspirational Studies. He had been a help in making me a part of the community, for he was both elegant and personable. He had helped me to befriend a number of people whom I otherwise might not have known. The whole town knew of his death and I now attended the Geyserville Chamber dinners alone.

I had started renting the rooms in the Lodge to groups. Various staff came and went, each with their own peculiarities. Some I enjoyed and others I wished never to see again.

I would still come and go from the city, for though I had sold my business, Juicy was supplying me with enamels as part of the pay back and these I still sold in my gallery. However, the gallery was starting to suffer as the designs became more and more diffused from the original ones. It was much less fun. I rented the factory building to a man who made honey and the Isis Street property to women who were starting in a business making maternity clothes. The purple house on Folsom now became my home in the city.

All the animals had moved to the country and I added to them a pony, a goat and a black sheep, I also got new peafowl, which I kept in a cage so they would be safe and not bother anyone by sitting on their cars, as they are prone to do. I added some colorful pheasants to the collection and some ducks and swans and Egyptian geese to the pond.

This pond had caused a problem while William was still alive. It had overflowed during some very heavy rains, due to over logging on the other side of the freeway. William was there to see me through the suit with the owners of that land and I won the case. He was there to see the pool redone and got to swim in it and use the hot tub that was built beside it. He was there as my first guests started to come, bit by bit. They would stay overnight in the Lodge and come down to breakfast in the big kitchen, where I had a long table with opera chairs from France placed around it. I bought a new Wolf range for the big kitchen and had the walk-in refrigerator refurbished. I called it the Isis Box.

The water situation was abominable in the beginning. It was from a well and full of iron so that everything became rusty. You could not drink this water at all, or wash your clothes in it for that matter. It was hard to resolve this but eventually I got city water with the help of my rather crazy plumber, Sir Chuck.

I managed to do much stained glass work and hired a helper that could assist me with this as well as the rooms that needed to be made up for guests. I learned how to cook at this time, not ever having been involved in that kind of domesticity before. I used to have instant coffee and remember the first day I had to open a coffee can in the big kitchen for some guests. I used a beer opener to make a hole, not realizing it was vacuum-packed, and the coffee jumped up and hit me in the eyes. It was very embarrassing. From that point I became very proficient in cooking breakfast and later lunches and dinners for various interesting groups that began to come to Isis Oasis.

I wanted to be like a mini Esalen and have workshops of some significance, not just a b&b for wine imbibers. That is why, one day, I was in my Gallery in San Francisco looking at the *Open Education Exchange* magazine, studying it for groups that might want to use Isis Oasis for their workshops. My eye fell upon an ad that described a man who had a Past Life Institute. His name intrigued me. It was Paul Ramses, and his address was just a block from my first Victorian house on Golden Gate Ave. Who could this be I wondered? I would have called but there was no phone number.

A few days later a friend of mine, Dion Dolphin, called me to talk to me about carrying a product in my shop, I had met her some time ago when I called her about an organization she belonged to. Her name interested me because my ex-husband had the same first name, just like the author Dion Fortune, who had inspired me to be involved with Isis and the occult world. Significant things always happen in threes.

This Dion worked with past lives and I asked her if she knew about the Past Life Foundation and specifically Paul Ramses. Surprisingly, she told me she knew him.

William Mitchell, a very elegant gentleman, 1979

Lora in the Theatre, imagining what might take place here, 1978

The pool and spa at Isis Oasis, 1979

CHAPTER VII

PAUL ENTERS MY LIFE

ion said she and Paul were doing some work together and would I like to meet him? I said I would, so she brought him over to visit me at the purple house. I thought he was quite an interesting person. I told him the story about Isis Oasis. We spoke of the possibility of creating a past life workshop there and began to put this in motion.

Time went by, with me coming and going from the country to the city, but the Gallery was losing its momentum. When the landlord doubled the rent, I opted out of the lease. No more Noir Gallery, no more factory, only money coming in from the rental of the two buildings and from Juicy paying in increments for the enamelcraft business.

It was a little scary, because Juicy was often late in his payments, but if he did not pay I would get his house, so in the end he paid me off.

I visited Dion Dolphin one evening because she was having a 106-year-old Huichol shaman at her home who was making a presentation. There was a small group of people sitting on the floor and I was sitting right behind Paul Ramses. It was around Halloween, I recall, because Paul consulted with me about a costume he was creating for a party he was attending. I remember wishing he would invite me, but he did not.

At the first of the year, it was time to move out of the Gallery, and I would need help. Dion suggested I call Paul Ramses. She said he was not presently working and needed some money. I called him and he pleasantly agreed. We spent several days loading up with all the materials from the store and chatted, getting to know each other better. When the van was packed to the gills, he suggested he might help me further by driving to Geyserville and unloading everything. I agreed, so on New Years Eve we drove to the country together.

Paul was delighted with my vision of Isis Oasis. After drinking a rusty nail at a bar in Healdsburg we decided to attend a party at the Odd Fellows Hall in the little town of Geyserville. We danced with each other while the townsfolk wondered who this stranger might be. They seemed to approve, however.

Paul was an attractive person with white hair and bright blue eyes. We were the same age, forty-eight, and neither of us had children, yet each of us had been married for twenty years and divorced.

Best of all, we both loved ancient Egypt. I discovered his name was not originally Paul Ramses. He had a short-lived marriage to a workshop leader, who had inspired him to change his name about a year ago. Since this recent marriage did not last he was single again.

We were both alone. It was inevitable that we should get together. Both of us had the sense that the Goddess willed it.

I was soon to leave for an Egyptian tour, so I arranged for Paul to watch Isis Oasis for me while I was away. The night before I left we spent together in the City and dined at the Castle Grand. We had our picture taken clinking glasses.

My two weeks in Egypt with an esoteric group, were filled with marvelous revelations, one after the other. Egypt felt to me, as it has for many who have traveled there, somehow familiar, like and old friend. I marveled at the temples, the pyramids and the tombs and from our learned guide discovered a lot more than I already knew about them. It was a wonderful trip and certainly enhanced my never-ending fascination with ancient Egypt,

Upon returning home, Paul met me at the airport. He was wearing a dark suit and holding a bouquet of flowers, which he handed to me before

embracing me. It felt good to have someone who
cared waiting for me, We went to the purple house
for the night. I had a large poster of a magician,
called Alexander, who resembled Paul. I had him
try on a makeshift turban and was amazed at
the remarkable similarity. It was as though our
togetherness was destined to happen, as this
poster came alive in him. As I gazed on him posing
as the magician, I recalled that long ago, a psychic
told me that my third relationship would be my
best and also my last.

Paul worked very well with the crew I had at Isis
Oasis and as I got good reports on his abilities, I
decided to make it more permanent and invited him
to come live at Isis. We picked up his belongings at
the bachelor pad he occupied in Berkeley. He had an
appointment in Calistoga that evening to facilitate
a past life session with a group of women. We all sat
in a circle as Paul worked his magic. We returned to
Isis Oasis through the wonderful winding Alexander
Valley Road.

This was the beginning of our life together.
We enjoyed the warmth of the fireplace in the old
house through the long, cold, winter. It was a time of
getting to know each other intimately.

When summer came, however, I discovered that
Paul could be very difficult. He was a drinker. At
one time he attended AA meetings, but gave it up.
His demeanor while drinking was sometimes caustic
and loud. He liked to argue and make an issue about

almost everything that I wished to do. It was very tiring. Of course, we had good times too, and I tried to deter him from this destructive behavior. He could be very charming and endearing, which made it difficult for me to want to divorce myself from him. I still hoped we could work things out.

I was taken aback when Dion Dolphin visited us and he went off with her to a room in the Lodge and made love to her. This he told me as he slipped into my bed at 2 a.m. I did not say anything, but just turned over. I was not happy, and it brought back bad memories. It changed our relationship forever, for it was a cruel act that caused a rift between me and Dion. We all went on an excursion the next day and it was very awkward for me to act normally. I suppose at this time in my life, it might not have mattered, but it did.

Our relationship deteriorated after that, with intermittent times of pleasure, especially when we went on vacation together. I thought maybe we should go to Egypt and see if it could heal the wounds I felt around his behavior, so I found a trip that included Greece, Egypt and Kenya on a safari.

We had a wonderful time. Paul could be a good companion and fun to travel with and the itinerary was spectacular. I introduced Paul to some of the Egyptians I had met on my earlier trip. We had special moments in our cabin while traveling by boat up the Nile that were unforgettable as we witnessed the amazing visions that appeared before our eyes. It was as though we traveled back in time.

Our visits to the other countries are also full of rich memories. I especially loved taking the night train to Mombassa as the sunrise appeared, watching the plains and herds of wildebeest, zebras, and giraffes. On safari in Nairobi, we viewed lions and cheetahs from a jeep, with our own private guide. All had been arranged for us, and we were the only ones on the tour. It was a dream come true and I thought it would bring us closer.

Upon returning to Isis Oasis, with the quick pace of keeping up with the guests and trying to juggle the staff, things between us became less than agreeable. Once again, rarely were my decisions accepted by Paul without an argument. He often became loud and verbally abusive. I managed to carry on and intermittently he could be helpful in ways that were valuable to me, and so we stuck it out.

Sometimes we would sit before our Isis altar together and put white light around the property and I would see the parts of Paul that I felt good about. He had the possibility of being the person I would like to live with. It was a familiar feeling, maybe something like what I experienced with my husband, Dion (another addictive personality). Often, women suffer similarly from one relationship to another. Is it the script for their lives? Many think so and it seems a cruel joke.

Paul only wanted to work on menial things, though I had imagined he would be leading groups doing the past life work that had intrigued me about him. He also chose whatever he wanted to do, not necessarily what was high priority, which made things chaotic and caused lots of anxiety for me. He often took exception to the staff, treating them in a way that would cause bad feelings. Then he would accuse me of being a poor manager.

Still, we carried on hosting different groups and having a myriad of experiences one could never have had with most life choices. Isis Oasis provided an amazing crucible for a rich and highly textured existence. No matter how difficult the group needs might be, we managed to always fulfill our obligation, often despite profound obstacles.

The staff also presented us with various problems for reasons that spanned the most outlandish scenarios, from attacking each other to leaving in the middle of the night with no notice. The buildings often needed repairs and the hot tubs were an endless source of distress with their tricks of not working just when they were needed the most. Paul tried to help with some of the problems, but usually only succeeded in creating more chaos.

I would try to find unusual events to attend. Once I discovered a very interesting ad in a free publication containing all kinds of classes. The ad described a Church known as the Union Temple of Isis. I determined to visit and Paul agreed to take me there. That is how I met Arisa and Dave, who conducted gatherings at their home in Oakland. We befriended them and through them discovered an organization called the Fellowship of Isis. The Isis manifestation at work again.

The Fellowship of Isis emanated from a castle in Ireland and was presided over by Lady Olivia and Lord Strathloch. I read their manifesto and readily connected with it. I decided to join the Fellowship of Isis and visit Clonegal Castle.

We made plans to travel, this time to Ireland, Spain, and Morocco. Once again we set off to journey together and see if things could be better if we were not wrestling with all the ups and downs of the retreat center business. We arranged to visit members of the Fellowship along the way. In Ireland Paul wanted to trace his family on his mother's side. My goal was to visit Clonegal Castle and meet Lady Olivia. I know the Goddess had her hand in this. She wanted me to follow the path that would lead me deeper into her service as a Priestess.

Paul and Lora in front of the Temple, 1983

Paul was an attractive person with white hair and blue eyes, 1981

We always enjoyed our times together when we traveled, 1985

Paul loved the animals at Isis Oasis, here with Loreon and two baby serval cats, 1986

DIARY *of* OUR VISIT *to* *the* FELLOWSHIP *of* ISIS

We are actually leaving Isis Oasis for a month, bouncing along the freeway, bound for San Francisco. It is a lovely sunny day, green hills, cows, wildflowers. There is nothing in my mind. All of our belongings are behind and hopefully being handled by Howard, my trusted young cousin, who is now working for us. There is always much to do at Isis Oasis and I hope he can handle it. We can but wait and see. This is a test of what might be. The Goddess is on our side and it's a great feeling.

It's been a long time since we flew away together, Paul and I, and what a struggle it has been to get through this period. We are finding our way. Searching for the answer to the rest of our lives.

Will we find it on this trip? Lord and Lady Strathloch await us in Clonegal Castle, Enniscorthy, Ireland.

Our plane was delayed one hour. We waited, discussing our itinerary: London for one night, an early trip to the British Museum, renting an auto and off to Stonehenge and parts west of England. Then we would follow the southern route to Hollyhead in Wales, and ferry across to Ireland. After spending St. Paddy's Day in Dublin, we would motor south to meet the Lord and Lady. We would tour Ireland for a few days before returning on the 24th of March to join in ritual at the Castle. After returning to England another way, we would leave from Heathrow to Spain and exotic Morocco.

Finally, we are off. First stop, Los Angeles and a free drink offered to appease the angry travelers. Our hope is to meet some fellow Isians along the way to discuss ideas and reasons for wanting to connect with the Goddess Isis.

Who knows, but that we may find someone who wishes to join us in our endeavors? On the other hand, we thought we might wish to relocate to a little island outside of Spain. We are going to investigate this, but I really think in my heart of hearts we will stay where we are and continue to do the work that the Goddess has assigned to us. We agree that the Earth is unbalanced and it is important to bring the feminine in balance with the masculine.

The plane is finally hurtling through the darkness over the land called Los Angeles. I reflect on spending 10 years of my life there and Paul reflects on spending 44 years in Chicago. We realize we are in a much better place and need to be thankful.

Our leaving Isis Oasis was hectic. The camera equipment that Paul was to handle just didn't come together. Our film bag was minus video cassettes and our tape machine was with us, but we didn't have any mikes. Paul worked on constructing a gate the day before we left. He was delayed by mowing a part of the property that could very well have been handled while we were gone. No amount of protesting on my part could dissuade him. This was typical of the problems happening frequently in our partnership.

The plane ride proved interesting in a synchronistic way. I sat next to a young women named Vivian, who was Stanley Kubrick's daughter and some of the Kubrick film *Barry Lyndon* was made at Clonegal Castle. Vivian Kubrick had been there when she was thirteen years old, and had met Lord and Lady Strathloch. She described her experience at the castle as being kind of scary. She was frightened when she and her sister were left in a room with Goddess images and an organ suddenly began to play mysteriously.

I spoke to her about their work with the Goddess and showed her their newsletter and a pamphlet written by Lady Olivia. Then I produced the photo that Olivia had sent me of the castle. On the back she had written that the edifice had been used in the film. Vivian said she would be interested in pursuing more information about the Fellowship.

She recognized the synchronicity.

We spoke of many things together: vegetarianism, healing, animals, the snakes in a Stephen Speilburg film and how they were mistreated, books, Mars and Venus. We spoke of the universal parental message "Be Careful" and the effect it had on children.

When we arrived at Heathrow, a woman from the seat behind told us of her interest in our esoteric conversation and that she was coming to London for a convention on crystals. She was from Nevada City and was into healing and the Goddess.

We caught a cab from the airport to the Kennedy Hotel, a rather conventional and more modern style place than we had expected to stay in London. Suffering from sleep depravation, we dozed off. When we woke it was too late to take in the theatre and have dinner, so instead we walked around to a pub. We met a gentleman from Sacramento, a travel agent. He suggested a number of things that we put on our itinerary.

Back at the hotel, we fell into a deep sleep, waking at ten, too late for breakfast so we walked for awhile until our appointment with David McDermott, a business associate of mine. After a pleasant chat and lunch at a charming pub (where we were joined by an English bulldog), we strolled to the British Museum and took in the Egyptian rooms until the museum closed. An occult bookshop run by the Theosophical Society was our next stop.

(As I write now it is a cold morning and we are at a little coffee house rearranging our trip. We have decided to fly to Dublin.)

We got to Dublin at two in the afternoon. Paul was upset at my process for making a decision or something I said or didn't let him say about spending money. We checked into Wynn's Hotel and had it out after he napped and I took a walk. A traumatic exchange, but we got through it. Perhaps we shall learn someday to consider each other's feelings more.

We arranged for dinner at Dobbin's, a barrel-shaped structure with red checked tablecloths and sawdust on the floor. We dined on pheasant and asked our charming waitress about things to do in the area. She suggested the Lower Deck as a place to visit after dinner, one of the many pubs. It was all Irish folk there, with nice young people who clapped and cheered and sang along with a very hot Irish band who garnished their performance with political statements.

By evening's end, Paul had consumed a goodly amount of beer interspersed with Irish Mist. He was in a playful mood and we took a bath together in the seven foot tub and made love with such ardor as had not happened in quite some time.

We got up very early in the morning to see about renting a car. We got somewhat hung up in the St. Paddy's Day parade route as we made our way to the Hotel Greshem, which had been suggested by an elderly fisherman we sat next to on the plane. It was lots fancier than Wynn's and we got a special room from which to view the parade. There were several families watching with us as we snapped photos and videod some of the highlights. It was interesting to note the general softness of the fathers with their children and the jolly good nature of the entire family. Oddly, one of the floats in the parade was by the Baha'i faith, proclaiming their message, "One Planet, One People, Please." I thought it significant.

We found a lunch spot that was not too crowded and decided on a nap before attending the National Concert Hall for a traditional Irish Music Program. We awoke feeling punk - too much drink last night. It's so easy to do here. The concert proved to be hundreds of children singing in chorus, Irish dancing featuring a nine-year-old girl and a young man playing the pipes, not to mention the Irish songs of an old lady and gentleman, both excellent, if you like that sort of thing and the Irish do, indeed. They are married to their culture and very nationalistic.

The next day we visited our first member of the Fellowship of Isis, Comtesse Joan de Frenay, a middle-aged nervous little women, like her two chow dogs. Her house, right across from the American Embassy, was in a good neighborhood but it seemed a little threadbare and messy. On her table were a bunch of bright yellow daffodils and some kind of leaves in a bowl, plus her set of Marseilles tarot cards. She didn't seem to want to socialize much and the phone took up some of her time. We learned that she was an early childhood friend of Olivia's and was into the occult before Olivia got involved. She was anxious to do the tarot for us. Paul opted out, so I got a reading. I didn't feel it was very insightful, but in the end I bought her tape and got the phone number of Lord and Lady Strathloch and we were off to our next adventure.

We visited Pat Griffin, an opposite type of person, very warm and jolly. Her rooms contained a massage table, several dogs, and lots of Chinese artifacts. The house looked out on the Irish Sea. We sat and talked for quite a while over coffee and cakes and knew here we had found a friend in Ireland.

Pat told us that, of course, there were a few nuts in the Fellowship and that they seemed to be attracted to that sort of thing, but there were many more who were authentic and genuinely good people with exceptional abilities. We took our leave of her with promises to meet again.

Next, we journeyed through the lovely green hills of the countryside to Wexford, where we found that we had gone too far. Earlier, we had stopped for soup and the waiter had suggested a wonderful hotel in Rossloe, so we made our way there. It had a sauna and a pool and many other amenities that we were delighted to take advantage of. After a fabulous dinner, I called the castle and talked to Olivia for the first time. We set up a luncheon date for Saturday. This allowed us more traveling time around Ireland, so we visited the towns of Wexford, Waterford and finally Cashel, where we stayed at Mrs. Foley's Bed

& Breakfast. We had dinner at the Bishop's Palace. It was a cold, blustery evening and we found it hard to stay warm.

The next day, after bidding Mrs. Foley a fond farewell, we journeyed to the towns of Limerick and then to Ennis. It continued gray and cold and I fell asleep waiting for Paul at the courthouse where he pursued his lost heritage.

We stopped at Bunnrady Castle with its Crafts Village and decided to dine there. The evening was fun and entertaining. We ate our dinner with our fingers with lots of wine and mead, interspersed with lovely song, harp and fiddle music.

We are back in our room on the Shannon River and Paul is sleeping. Earlier today I asked him to use a spell to dispense anger. I gave him a black rock I had found along the way and asked him to put his anger into it and throw it in the river, but it did not work. On the way home from our delightful evening, I found occasion to point out the need for him to watch the road, as four people were walking in it while he was fiddling with the radio. I could feel his anger returning and it is there now as he sleeps; the anger of a young boy controlled by mommy. When will men see that they do not have all the answers?

Tomorrow we have an appointment with Sean O'Driscoll at Castle Matrix, who Olivia had referred us to and who is a member of the Fellowship of Isis.

We awoke to grayish skies, but not too dreary, and a cheery breakfast with our hostess and some other guests. We soon were on our way via a very green and wonderful countryside with ruins all along the way. We found the castle down a lane of yew trees with a ram standing sentinel. We knocked upon the heavy wooden door. It opened suddenly and a tiny fellow came out, quite startling both of us.

Sean O'Driscoll started to tell us about his castle almost at once. He was clearly a very proud owner. Once an American, he was a long time expatriate, having lived in Paris and now Ireland. He invited us inside and we chatted about Irish history, Goddesses and heraldic symbols.

Elizabeth, lady of the castle, came in and we spoke with her for awhile before she left to feed the goats. O'Driscoll told us he had been with her for four years and, though she had been told she could never have children, after being in the castle, a baby was born to her.

He showed us around the castle, where each room had been done in just the right way with just the right decorations, He told us about buying the library cabinets, which arrived with some rare books in a secret panel that turned out to be worth the cost of the cabinet. The Sir Walter Raleigh statue he had insured for over the amount of its cost and got broken enroute, thereby being essentially free. The altar he found at a Paris flea market was being used as a food stand. He managed to purchase it as he recognized it as very precious.

Finally he told us about the bell, which he

bought on a whim ten years before he had the castle and just fit in the bell tower which had no bell when he moved in. He led us up the steep narrow stairs to the belfry. As he walked through the door at the top of the tower he cautioned us to lower our heads. He himself fitted perfectly through the portals.

Here was a man who manifested many marvels most successfully. A lifelong collector of historic objects, he found the perfect castle as a repository. He had a woman and a baby to share it with and had started the Heraldic Society. As we left, I remarked at his ability to get it all together and he gave me a wink and said, "You see, there really is magic!"

We were delighted with our visit and waved goodbye to Sean, his wife Elizabeth, and their dog, as they stood outside their castle door.

We then pressed on to Cork, after a stop in Limerick to pick up the battery for the camera, driving through tidy town, after tidy town with wonderful children, red-cheeked, happy, healthy, and also friendly and well-behaved. We got advice from various wonderful characters as we asked directions.

We arrived in Cork, a charming town, and checked into the Metropole, a fine ancient hotel. We dined at the oyster bar on great oysters, scampi, scallops and a host of veggies. Then we went out to Bluebrook Castle and a rocking Irish Band.

After a good night's sleep, we went for a tour of the city, truly a fabulous place on the Lee River, with bridges and antiquated buildings everywhere.

We visited Blarney Castle, climbing step after step, shivering against the freezing cold castle walls, and kissed the Blarney Stone. Now we shall be forever eloquent. We found the museum after a great deal of difficulty, but part of the experience here is asking directions as often as possible.

To get to Buncloudy before dark was impossible, so we stopped at Waterford and took a room in the old hotel overlooking the river. After a scrumptious meal of roast beef and Yorkshire pudding, we retired early.

We started off at daybreak and would have arrived in time if we didn't get off on a wild goose chase trying to find Kavenaugh's, an unmarked bed and breakfast, and then taking a few wrong turns.

Finally there it was: Clonegal Castle. We drove around to the back courtyard and went up to the door over which was a bas relief of Isis. We knocked loudly as suggested by a sign on the door. It was opened slowly by Lawrence, Lord Strathloch, I presumed.

His hat was stiff with age and tattered and split up the back. His coat was scruffy and tied with a string and his black suit beneath was a baggy antique. But his face was that of a pontiff: at first rigid, but softening more and more as we spoke with him.

Olivia joined us in the drawing room. I stood up and gave her a little hug, which I think startled her. Her eyes startled me. They were indeed quite crossed as we had been told they would be, but she had a lovely welcoming smile. I imagined her eyes could see things that were obscured to most people.

We all sat huddled near the fire for warmth and talked animatedly about our various backgrounds, and of course, Isis. We were joined by a young man, David, a sculptor and nephew and Poppy, Lady Stratlock, a frail sweet elderly woman with crutches, who after having several strokes was left a little palsied.

Lawrence put logs on the fire while Olivia asked quick questions without, many times, waiting for answers. At length we were ushered into the dining room where two places were set at the end of the table. "Paul is to sit at the head," said Olivia. We were offered home made wine. She then summoned our meal through a hole in the fireplace. It was put on a trolly which fitted into the opening of the hearth. Lawrence and Olivia hadn't waited to lunch with us, as they said they were busy with their flag being installed on the roof.

The conversation centered on members of the Fellowship of Isis until Olivia said she must lie down a bit and bade Lawrence to take us on a tour. A small dog joined us. Lord Strathloch put a loose leather loop over the dog's head, which continually came off, but the dog went along anyway.

We walked around the castle to the twelfth century "ruined" abby. Lawrence spoke slowly and quietly with pride of the beautiful aging castle and how lovely it was in the spring.

Strolling through the yew tree walk between the walls of entwined trees with marvelously gnarled trunks, we spoke of the magic of trees. He pointed to the wilderness area and the place where the river ran through the 150 acre estate. We peered into the greenhouse filled with plants, an office cluttered with a kiln and pottery shards, and the stables, now a storehouse.

Again in the castle proper we were led into a room with a number of stuffed antique animal heads, among them an entire alligator with marble eyes. Beyond that was the loo, a room with an aged toilet. Clocks hung from pegs in hallways with artwork great and small and tapestries in various stages of decay. We stopped to admire a rather grand bedroom done up with a fabulous Egyptian-style four poster bed (fourteenth century, he told us).

The library was the most rare of all, with ancient books reaching to the ceiling on all four walls. A huge desk was in the center and some comfortable chairs were arranged near the fireplace. The vast window framed a garden scene outside, all so incredibly aged. I could imagine Lord Strathloch sitting here for hours, writing his detailed books and utilizing the amazing reference material in the huge collection of literature lining the walls.

We then climbed up, to, and through, a dusty attic to the turret where the new flag, blue ground with yellow castle symbol, flew at the corner. We went through a tiny window and hoisted ourselves out onto the leaden roof to see the lovely green scenery surrounded by smooth snow-laden mountains.

Back down to the courtyard, we were invited to

wander about until five, when we should meet for tea. The sun came out a bit, so Paul and I strolled about with the video camera, filming the wonderful places we had just seen.

Tea with Olivia occurred in a tiny room with a small heater while she watched Dr. Who on the telly. We chatted amicably and watched the show with her.

At length we left for dinner in Kavenaugh's dining room, still pinching ourselves to see if what we experienced was real. We had a return appointment tomorrow at two for a ritual. Paul and I decided to take a mind altering pill called "adam," which we thought would enhance the experience.

Morning came and we made ready to leave Kavenaugh's for a ride up the mountain. There was still snow on the peaks and the scene was magnificent, as the green faded into a white landscape. Two dray horses grazed on the side of the road and several hang gliders wafted overhead, a tribute to the fact that the human being is ever reaching out to fly like a bird or a god.

We returned to the village and took our pills in a pub with some hot tea. Then we drove to the castle a different way from the day before. From this elevation we could see it tucked within a stand of trees, the land around it plus the town and the wondrous green hills. We arrived at the castle on the dot of two and were granted an audience for video filming with Lawrence and Olivia before we met in the dining room where a number of people were assembling. Soon a procession to the temple of Isis began winding down into the bowels of the castle.

Here was a world of magic and mystery. There were twelve altars signifying each zodiac sign and a stage with artifacts of ancient Druidic and Celtic origins. Old Egyptian tapestries lined the walls. When I looked within a crystal ball over Brigid's Well, at the heart of the castle, I saw a vision of the world with a peaceful aura. We lit a candle and made a wish together. We looked out a magic window, to the left for our past, and the right for our future. The mirrors on each side echoed off into infinity.

Olivia proclaimed the spring (it being a celebration for the Vernal Equinox) and ordained several people from the order of the Golden Morn. Then to our surprise she announced others might give readings, including Paul and me. I had my crystal wand and did a ritual summoning the Goddesses to be with us from all directions, each signifying a different season. Later we did in fact see the seasons change before our eyes in a matter of moments, when the courtyard was delightfully filled with hail stones that danced magically on the castle grounds, whereas it had been sunny a moment ago.

We sat on wonderful stuffed snakes that wrapped themselves around the pillars of the temple as Paul took us into a past life, a guided tour starting with the throne of forgiveness. We then did a snake dance singing "We are the Old People, We are the New People, We are all people, deeper than before."

When the ritual was over we adjourned to the kitchen with its giant old stove and boxes of veggies stacked up. The huge table was laden with foodstuffs and bottles of wine and we all sat around and spoke of magic and Aleister Crowley, Dion Fortune, the Goddess, and tales that Olivia told one after the other in rapid and humorous vein.

The hours drifted by and it was growing dark when we took leave, and hugged Lord Strathloch and Lady Olivia and some of the others goodbye. The moon was out lighting the beautiful trees silhouetted against a colorful night sky. Lord Strathloch walked with us and as we passed the well I asked if I could take some of the sacred water with me, which he allowed.

Pinching ourselves once again, totally awed that we had been a part of what we experienced that afternoon, we agreed it would have been just as wonderful without the "adam."

We reached Dublin several hours later to spend a comfortable night at the Gresham Hotel before flying off to England to view Stonehenge and Avesbury. There we visited a few members of the Fellowship of Isis, notably a man called Charles Shepherd. He lived in a lovely little cottage so typical of the English countryside. He sat with us for tea in his cozy living room and told us of his time as a student of Dion Fortune. It was thrilling to meet one with such a background.

He showed us his garden, of which he was rightly proud. It was a series of altars based on the work of

Rudolph Steiner. He gave me the name of a woman in Santa Rosa, California, Moyae Kennedy, with whom he corresponded regularly. (Today she is one of the Priestesses of the Temple of Isis.) After hearing about Isis Oasis, he advised me to build a Temple on the grounds.

Charles Shepherd was certainly an influential wizard. Upon returning home, we did indeed build a Temple - or rather it manifested. The vision just materialized along with the intent. It was like Lord Strathloch had said: "You just have to be receptive and meet the Goddess halfway." Her intent was to have a Temple and we did what was needed to create it.

I had heard about a theatre in Oakland with an Egyptian motif. I went there and found that the man responsible had a workshop in Oakland called "Whatever Works." We got lots of plaster pieces with hieroglyphs, bas reliefs and Egyptian pillars which we applied to the frame of the Temple. I painted the whole thing in wonderful colors, just as the temples had been painted thousands of years ago. On a black ceiling I painted an astrology wheel in gold, using the symbology of the temple at Dendara in Egypt. The inside was painted with stylized lotus and depictions of Isis, Osiris, Maat and symbols of many kinds. A table with a marble top materialized for the altar. Other pieces of sculpture I had collected completed the whole effect and shelves on all four corners depict the four directions with appropriate sacred objects.

This Prayer is kept in our small Temple for all to use.

PRAYER TO ISIS

*Divine Isis, Goddess of ten thousand names, I invoke your grace...
come to our temple oh Goddess, dwell in our shrine. Make our hearth
your altar, our hearts your home, bring vision and healing to those
who use this shrine, give us wisdom and unveil the truth, and with
thy feathery wings protect us, breathe into us the breath of life and
health and strength.*

*Let us honor the direction of the East...element of air, which brings
us intelligence and lightness of being , borne out by the birds
that fly on the winds ever blowing. (breathe deeply and feel the
universal gift of life.)*

*Let us honor the direction of the South...element of fire, which brings
us love and brightens our path with its flames ever glowing...(visualize
your internal flame deriving energy from its light.)*

*Let us honor the direction of the West...element of water, which
cleanses and purifies us and brings us intuition and depth like the
oceans,lakes and rivers ever flowing... (use this element now to
open your third eye.)*

*Let us honor the direction of the North...element of Earth which
brings us nourishment and abundance and provides us our home and
all the animals, tress and plants with their seeds ever growing...(taste
the fruit, smell the flowers, touch the crystal.)*

*We come into this world with all these gifts, and more, our very
own special essence...let us thank the Goddess for that which she
bestows...let us go forth refreshed and renewed with dedication to
preserve and respect all life, for we are all children of Isis, the great
mother Goddess!*

Loreon and Charles Shepard, formerly a student of Dion Fortune

Loreon on the roof of Clonegal Castle with Lawrence (Lord Strathloch) and the new flag

Loreon and Lord Strathloch in front of the Abby

Loreon and Lord Strathloch in front of Clonegal Castle

Lord and Lady Strathloch performing a ritual

NEAR DEATH *and* BEYOND

*P*aul and I took many other trips after that to India, Sri Lanka, Nepal, Bali, Philippines, Singapore, Indonesia, Belize, Canada, Mexico, Costa Rica, lots of places in the U.S. too. Our travels added a lot of richness to our lives. Venturing forth into other countries and meeting people from different cultures is an important part of our understanding of the world and each other. I am very thankful I have been able to have those experiences.

Most of the time, though, we were caught up working on Isis Oasis and facilitating groups as they came and went. There were weddings, family gatherings, bicycle groups, yoga groups, theatre groups, tantra groups, Stan Grof's holotropic breathing, Natalie Roger's expressive therapy,

David Quigley's alchemical hypnotherapy, Amron mystery school and on and on.

In 1983. after our trip to Ireland, Lady Olivia wrote to me. I can remember sitting on a bench under the ancient fir tree reading her letter. She asked if Paul and I would like to become Priestess and Priest of the Fellowship of Isis. We were surprised and pleased and quick to reply that we would. We choose the historical date of the marriage of Isis and Osiris, July 19th.

The ceremony took place in attunement with Castle Clonegal in Ireland. We performed the ritual in the Theater with Arisa and Dave, of the Union Temple of Isis, to assist us in our vows. Another priestess of the Fellowship also appeared, as though by magic, and one of the staff was on hand to be the scribe. We had recently emptied the pool and refilled it with fresh water, so after the ceremony Paul and I were the first to step into the clear, sparkling pool. And so it was done. It felt like a very important ritual, as the cause of honoring the Goddess in her rightful place became our focus thenceforth.

Running a retreat center is not easy. One has to make sure all rooms are made up properly for the guests and that the meeting areas are arranged as required. Menus must be written and food purchased, cooked and served on time. It required more helpers as we got busier and Isis Oasis became a more lively center. I rarely had any time to devote to myself or to indulge in my artwork. I told myself Isis Oasis was itself a living art project, and the guests supported this idea by praising the beauty of the space. This sufficed to keep us forever improving and beautifying the grounds and buildings.

Paul and I continued to disagree on many things. If I liked a staff person, he did not. If I booked a group, he might not want that group to come. If I made a decision about how to do something, he would find fault. This constant differing of opinions made work at Isis Oasis less than the wonderful experience it might have been.

We lived in the wine country and Paul would often drink too much. This would make him impossible and our arguments grew and gave me much cause for unhappiness. I no longer felt much support from him and began to feel hopeless. I distanced myself and wished he would leave. As time passed, he spent more time in the city and I assumed more responsibility at Isis Oasis.

Once, when I had a huge wedding scheduled, he was not at Isis Oasis, having gone to an event in the city. It felt unfair to me and then felt worse when he called to ask me if I could guess whose bed he was sleeping in that night. I was surprised that he could be so glib about a matter like that. Of course, I had no idea. He told me that he was at the home of Gail Love, a woman who I knew about, but did not know personally. She ran a mystery school and was well known in the New Age community. He told me it was nothing intimate, but he had met her at the gathering and offered to help her with something at her house. When it got late, he was asked to stay. This did not sit well with my psyche and I fretted about it, especially in light of all the hard work I had to do while Paul was playing around in the city.

The next day I washed and dyed my hair. I liked to keep my hair as black as possible and the gray was beginning to show. Paul was coming back and we were scheduled to go out to dinner and a play. I put on my makeup and observed the effect of my black hair and kohl-lined eyes. I could pass for an Egyptian, I thought. I wondered what Gail Love looked like.

When Paul did show up, I acted as if nothing had happened and asked no questions, but I can remember wondering what went on with his new friend. I was harboring lots of resentment. We got ready to go out. On the ride to Jenner, which is on the coast, we purchased a television for our bedroom. Then we had a tasty dinner at Murphy's Jenner-by-the-Sea Restaurant and went to the play, a delightful rendition of *Fiddler on the Roof.*

On the way home, once again I would have liked to find out more about his new liaison, but I said nothing. When we got back it was late. Paul insisted on carrying the large box containing the TV up the stairs, even though he had a weak back and often had to go to a chiropractor. I protested, asking him to wait for morning when he could get help, but to no avail.

That night at the stroke of midnight, just after

getting in bed, I began to feel very ill. Paul made light of it and did not do much to help at first, but he was a witness to my distress. He brought me some tea and antacid, thinking I had indigestion. In the night, I got out of bed and fainted. After awhile, I do not know how long, I woke and found my black dog lying in front of me in the exact pose one sees of the jackal guardian god Anubis. I remember thinking that Anubis had guided me back to life from the nether world.

There were high ferns on either side of the claw foot bathtub which rested on a dais in the center of our large bathroom, I recall clearly that I fainted once again, this time amongst the ferns, but instead of blackness I saw light. It glowed and a white form beckoned me to come forth. I was totally unafraid. A feeling of peace and warmth came over me. I surrendered to whatever might be my fate. From this state I rose once again. Apparently, it was not my time. I managed to get back in bed and slept till morning.

When I awoke I realized I must call my doctor and tell him what had occurred. He summoned me to his office immediately and I recounted my experience. My doctor declared that I had suffered a heart attack. I was dumbfounded, never having imagined anything was the matter with my heart. I was then taken by ambulance to a hospital for an angioplasty, which unclogged the blood clot that had caused the attack.

After a few days I returned home, restored,

although part of my heart had died. I could not help thinking that perhaps the attack was brought on because of the distress I was feeling about the situation with Paul. About a week after this incident, I went to a healing circle to see a well-known shaman woman. Paul drove me there and, oddly, the first person we saw was Gail Love. I had wanted to meet her after the incident with Paul, and so she appeared. Not all that attractive I thought, but no doubt an interesting person. I suppose it was strictly platonic, but still I resented Paul for helping her instead of being at Isis Oasis during a time when a big event was taking place.

After my heart attack everything seemed to be glowing with vitality and I was glad to still be a part of it. I had experienced altered states of many kinds. I had known poverty and incarceration first hand. I had known the feeling of betrayal every women has when her man turns to someone else for intimacy. I had known death and near-death. Though I had never been a mother, my nurturing instincts were satisfied by nursing baby ocelots and serval cats. Though I rarely suffered illness, I occasionally experienced sudden problems. Once I had a painful gall bladder attack that required an operation, and later a badly broken ankle taught me the difficulties of what it is like to not be able to walk.

When one's life has been threatened, one begins to appreciate everything. I wanted to sit out under the giant tree and observe the beauty of nature even more. It wasn't long before I resumed my life, doing things pretty much the same as always, yet I knew that my heart had to be acknowledged and protected.

Through correspondence, I met Murry Hope, who was the closest living person to the author Dion Fortune. She offered to do a workshop at our center. This was one of the first workshops I put on myself, making posters and flyers and sending invitations out to a list she sent me. When Paul and I picked Murry and her husband up at the airport, we became immediate friends and had much to discuss that was stimulating and fascinating.

The workshop was a success. Murry was wonderful in her delivery of occult knowledge, which seemed to pour out of her. I had bought a lot of her books to sell during her time here and most did. Murry and I continued to stay in touch and she came back again for another workshop the very next year. But life is ever-changing and the last time I heard from Murrry, she was having a divorce, suffering illness and had written a new book called *The Changeling*. She indicated that she and I no longer had much in common and I suspected that she had turned toward a more conventional philosophy. We have not corresponded since.

We decided to put on a convocation for the Fellowship of Isis. We invited Olivia, but she declined, saying she did not like to fly. A priestess with the Fellowship, Morgan le Fey, from Georgia attended. She was very knowledgeable and well-versed in all the liturgy of the Fellowship, having spent a lot of time at Clonegal Castle. She suggested we ordain those in attendance if they wished to be. We thereupon ordained seventeen people in a ceremony under the big tree. This event was on the front page of the *San Francisco Chronicle* with photos, as they happened to be doing a story on Isis Oasis that weekend.

Morgan felt certain that Lady Olivia and Lord Strathloch would be most appreciative of this mass ordination, in that each person seemed so worthy of the honor. However, Olivia did not take kindly to it and would not send the certificates to the newly-ordained unless they happened to be members of the Fellowship prior to the gathering, which only a few were. So I issued certificates from the Isis Society for Inspirational Studies to those who were ordained.

One person, who had not wished to be part of the ordination ceremony, later reconsidered, so we did a ritual for her in the small meditation temple. She choose to serve Ixchel, Mayan rainbow Goddess. This new priestess came to visit often, until one day she was found dead in her apartment. Her children brought her ashes to be placed under a tree at Isis Oasis.

Lady Olivia did eventually come and visit. Her brother Lawrence, Lord Strathloch, had died and she decided to brave the flight and tour the U.S.A. All was in readiness for her arrival and we had a marvelous time with her. We performed plays in the theatre and with Olivia pranced about one evening, which, considering her age was quite remarkable.

I took Olivia to San Francisco and drove her to the ocean, where we wrote cryptic messages in the sand and watched the waves pour over them, washing our magical writings out to sea. Together we spoke of ways to have the Fellowship grow, as well as making Isis Oasis a center for the Goddess. Olivia, being very wise, shared her wisdom with us freely. Her energy flowed from every pore of her small body and her amazing power was felt by all.

I had arranged for her to give a talk at the Amron Center, a metaphysical church run by some very wonderful people, Norma Tringali, and her mate Edmond. They brought many profound programs to the public absolutely free and they were always having financial problems as a result. Norma used Isis Oasis as a retreat for her residential mystery school. After her death I was sad to hear the church had folded without her. I began to contemplate my own mortality, including questioning how my own legacy might play out.

At one point during the earlier years at Isis Oasis, Dion's mother came back into my life. We had not spoken since the time Dion was in a coma in the hospital in San Francisco. Gone was the great beauty she had always been. Alas, personal beauty is such a fleeting thing. Mother Nature imposes wrinkles and gray hair no matter how you fight it. Even at eighty years old, Dorothy would put the yellow of an egg on her face every day, hoping to ward off old age. It wasn't working, unfortunately. She called me after her husband Harry died quite suddenly during surgery, and she was left all alone.

Paul and I went to visit her at her house in Pacifica. She had become quite eccentric, with over thirty cats living with her. Needless to say she was not able to keep things very tidy or odor free. It was near impossible to stay in her house for any length of time. She had a collection of Dion's art on her grimy walls. Looking at them, I was awash in nostalgia. I asked what had happened to Dion's ashes. When we were young and so connected, Dion and I envisioned we would be in vases next to each other on a mantle somewhere. She told me that she had scattered the ashes in the woods. I felt bereft, knowing that Dion would have wanted me to be involved in the care of his remains.

We helped Dorothy by getting her a lawyer who worked on the case of her husband, as he should not have died on the operating table. She eventually received $50,000, which aided her significantly for a time. We helped her to get a hearing aid and invited her to stay with us at Isis Oasis on occasion. One day she confessed to me that she actually still had Dion's ashes. We arranged for her to bring them to Isis Oasis.

There were two gay men who had befriended Dorothy when she was more spry. She had met them through her cat rescue work. They brought her over with the ashes one day and helped me to plant a fir tree over them, beside the Temple at the entrance to Isis Oasis, so that all who enter must pass the tree.

It has comforted me many times, as I can hold its

branches and inquire of it when I am unsure of my next step. William's tree is over the bridge and this, too, is useful when there are things I know he would take an interest in and be helpful with. I am now looking at where my tree should be, as I am convinced that this is a good method of in some way remaining present. Even if no one knows your ashes are there, you will always be beautiful and provide shade and homes to birds who will alight on your branches.

The men moved Dorothy into a house next door to them and saw to her as best they could. Eventually she had to go to a rest home and give up all her cats. It was there that she died in her nineties. I called to inquire about Dion's artwork. They told me they had all been destroyed in the basement during a flood. Nothing was left, but Dion never completely disappeared from my life.

When I first had Isis Oasis an incident happened that was most unusual. Dion's heroin connection was a dealer named Cowboy, a black man who was so well known for his dealing dope that a play had been written about him. I remember seeing the play in the city during the Beatnik days. Soon after Dion's death, the Baha'i people had a reunion at Isis Oasis.

I was quite pleased about this, as the land had been theirs for seventy years and I was eager to learn more about their philosophy. When they started to arrive, who should I see walking across the lawn, but Cowboy.

"What are you doing here?' I asked suspiciously. I was very cold and distant as I considered him an enemy.

"I have become a Baha'i and it has changed my life," he answered.

The strangeness of the situation amazed me and I could only soften my feelings for this person. I welcomed him and we spoke of Dion's demise. I wondered if he was the man who brought Dion to the hospital, but I never asked him that question. I couldn't help thinking it would have been so good if Dion had found a path that would have allowed him to give up heroin. He could have been here with me, helping to grow Isis Oasis.

Often I would come across a book or a card that had Dion's writing on it. He would put down ideas or inventions inside book jackets and in little booklets he would make by hand that also often contained intricate drawings. I still had a closet full of some historic tapes he had made and films he had worked on.

Quite a while later, a couple got married at Isis Oasis who were 16 mm film buffs. They knew all about the film scene in the 50s and the various artists who participated in it. They showed films during their reception and they discovered that I had been associated with the experimental film movement. They lived close to me in the city, so I arranged to give them Dion's material, since they had the equipment to examine it. This they did, and invited me to see the collection of films that Dion had made. It was a potpourri of familiar images. They had also tapes of interviews which such luminaries as Alan Watts, Jordan Belson and Alan Ginsburg, whom Dion would tape along with his camera to capture some of the special happenings of that time. The documentaries have now become valuable archives of that era.

I gave a television station some of Dion's filmwork and they used it in a piece they did on San Francisco in the 50s. Ironically, more recognition came to Dion long after his death, as this couple worked successfully to place the films in collections at the San Francisco Museum of Modern Art and at a film retrospective at the Whitney Museum in New York.

I also gave them the manuscript that Dion's mother had written. It was a complete book about her son, dealing primarily with his drug habit. She saw his use of heroin as an illness and was always very accepting of it, unlike me. I could not fathom allowing this substance to destroy all that creativity and his ability to live with one he had vowed to love. Eventually this couple presented all the tapes, film and the book to the Pacific Film Archive in Berkley, where it shall remain.

Now here I am, like Dorothy, growing old, working on my biography, contemplating life. It is as though I were dying and all that made up my existence on this planet is passing through my brain. Memories seem to be made up of the most ecstatic moments and the most painful. Past lives are often memories of death in another time and another place in another body...

Paul and I went to Chicago for the Parliament of World Religions 100th anniversary gathering.

We were in a play Lady Olivia had written in which the Earth and the Moon became united after the planets and the constellations chastised Earth for his many improper acts and he finally transforms. The Goddess Isis and other ritualistic features were part of the play. At the last minute, a harpist I had met joined our group and played for the performance, making it quite professional. It was a great success.

The entire event was wonderful. The Pagan presenters got a lot of publicity as they performed all together at a full moon ceremony in the park. Lady Olivia was among the notables that spoke to the large audience with a simple but energetic and meaningful address that caused others who came on stage afterward to include the Goddess, along with God, in their speeches.

After the Parliament, I met Paul's family, for they all lived in Chicago where he grew up. That night I had a painful attack that proved to be gallstones and I ended up in the hospital, though I was able to fly home for an operation in our local hospital.

About this time, Paul was becoming ill and would sit for days and brood in the bedroom, locked away from all activity. I continued, bravely, to run things at Isis Oasis with the help of the staff. We kept up the aging property and I made lots of new women friends, all women who connected with the Goddess. We created a Wise Woman's Circle that met weekly, and began regular Full Moon Ceremonies, where Diveena, a lovely young priestess, would preside.

When I was 60 I changed my name to Loreon. I awoke one day with that name on my tongue. I realized it was a combination of *Lora* and *eon*, and since I was always fond of studying ancient legends it seemed most appropiate.

Isis Oasis was becoming the mystical place I wished it to be. I continually found ways to enhance the buildings, and visitors always marveled at the attention to detail. Everywhere you turned there was a statue, a bas-relief, a stained glass window to remind you of ancient Egypt. Artifacts kept manifesting for me, which always surprised me, but then the Goddess was on my side, guiding me, of that I was certain. I was making Isis Oasis a living museum, and by doing so, keeping the memory of an amazing old culture alive.

I was given guidelines, by the Goddess, about how this was to be done. First there was the breath of Isis that came to me. I was instructed to engage in a new form of breathing whereby one breathes in to "Inner Sanctum" and exhales to "Infinite Space". Note that these words start with the initials I S I S. I discovered that this breathing technique was a great help to clear the mind for meditation.

Then there was "neter yoga", a form of body movement that expressed the attributes of the deities of ancient Egypt. This would allow a participant to take on the powers of the multiplicity of the various Goddesses and Gods of that time.

A greeting that could take the place of shaking hands or bowing in the prayer position came to me.

It was holding both hands up in the praise position upon meeting another, then holding them out to feel the aura of the other person, who would do the same, and finally ending with the hands crossed over the heart while saying "Baraka".

As far as name changing, I encourage it. Your name or Ren, as the Egyptians called it, signified your identity. It was one of the nine bodies that they knew as the Shenkas. There was the Ka, your outer self; the Ba, your inner self; the Sahu or soul; the Khu, a spark within the soul; the Ab or heart, the seat of our emotions; the Kahbit or shadow self; the Sekhem or life force; and the Khat which is the human body. It is a kind of chakra system that allows us to know ourselves, know our soul, know our hearts, and know our purpose, which is taken from the wisdom of the ancient ones.

The Retreat House

Olivia in our small temple, visiting Isis Oasis for the first time, 1995

The small ornate Temple we built, with visiting harpist

The first ordinations at Isis Oasis, 1990
Left to right: Vicki, Edith, Morgan, Loreon, Paul, Diane, Coro, Otter, Morning Glory

NINE PRIESTESSES
in EGYPT

*T*he seed of the visitation to the land of Egypt was incubating.

I was laid up with a broken ankle brought about by an incident with my Egyptian geese. They normally resided in the pond, but they decided one day to take a walk to town. Seeing this and fearing for their demise, I tried to herd them home by putting on my purple boots and a burst of speed to head them off. It was the proverbial wild goose chase! I fell as I rounded a corner and discovered I could not get up. My ankle was clearly broken. At the hospital it was revealed it was a double break and needed an immediate operation. I would be unable to walk for three months.

While convalescing, a friend visited and

suggested we go on a trip to Egypt at the end of the year. I wondered if I could be walking well enough by then, but as the time progressed I began to move about without my walker, almost without being gimpy, and so we planned our trip.

Egypt had been my destination three times before, but it was never enough to satisfy my wonder and awe of what the ancient ones had created, so I was looking forward to being there once again. Soon a group of women formed, all priestesses who also felt the time was right to go, until there were nine of us planning to go together.

Just a week before the trip, I fell at the base of the stairs in the old house and I severely injured my foot and toe, opposite to the ankle that had been broken. I spent a miserable night unable to sleep because of the pain, wondering if I could walk well enough to make the journey. The next day I determined not to see the doctor and just simply willed myself to be healed.

I delivered three baby serval cats to the airline with a ticket for Texas, where a person I knew was to pick them up and find good homes for them. I always find competent and experienced people for the cubs born at Isis Oasis and it was always hard saying goodbye to the adorable babies as I watched them in their carrier ready to fly.

I thought back to some of the strange events that happened to me before I left. Three lights had burnt out within an hour of each other as I walked from room to room. Then, as I was about to pack my travel alarm clock I dropped it, causing it to break. When I got to San Francisco I purchased another one only to discover it was defective and no figures appeared on its face. Also, just before I left Isis Oasis I stopped at the temple to commune with the Goddess Isis, and ask for blessings for the trip. As I left the temple to get into the car, I noticed the two Egyptian geese walking around the grounds far from the pond and looking very smug. There was no time for me to chase them back into their enclosure at the pond, and besides my days of running after them was over, so I just had to leave them to their fate

At the airport I sat with Carolyn, who was on the staff at Isis Oasis and had been ordained a Priestess of Isis of 10,000 names when Lady Olivia had been visiting Isis Oasis just a few weeks before. Mother of two children who had recently left home to venture on their own, Carolyn had decided to establish herself at the Isis Center because of her devotion to the Goddess. For this trip she carried with her an autoharp, a basket of clothes, and a tiny suitcase. Her hair was braided in the manner of a little girl and her country attire and way of speaking signified her southern background. Soon Caite, Priestess of Sekhmet, whom I had ordained last year, appeared, charming and sprightly as usual and armed with a suitcase full of books and ritual objects. B.J. greeted us with her deep masculine voice. She was our oldest member, being in her seventies, with snow-white hair, yet still very spry and going for her Ph.D. in anthropology at U.C. Berkeley. She had been ordained at Isis Oasis five years before as Priestess of Hecate. The beautiful dancer, Elizabeth, was next to show, as always perfectly attired, looking like a biblical figure. It was fitting that she chose Mary Magdalene as her deity at her ordination. Finally Sophia, striking and voluptuous, appeared. She kissed her consort goodbye just as we were boarding the plane. Being a cat woman, she was dubbed Priestess of Bast at her ordination by Lady Olivia.

All of us were connected by our association with the Honorable Olivia Robertson, who carried on her astonishing work with Goddess energy and the Fellowship of Isis, laying a foundation for the shift to the feminine emanating on the planet at this time. I have come to believe this is one of the most important movements of our era. We boarded our plane.

From my window seat, the scenery was magnificent. It was a fabulous day to fly. The city looked so tiny and fragile as we passed over it and the silver of the waterways sparkled like shiny ribbons along the landscape of the Earth. As we headed toward Los Angeles, misty mountains floated above rugged terrain topped by fluffy clouds. It wasn't long before we began to descend into the midst of L.A. and made the transfer to Egypt Air. We boarded with great anticipation, though part of me wondered why I was going and the other part was filled with excitement to discover more and experience a greater depth to my understanding of that ancient land. This part longed to set foot on the sacred ground once more. I knew that I was to use this time to begin to fathom how the rest of my life will be played out, looking now at the twilight of my years. I had decisions to make. I looked out the window of the plane and saw we were flying into the darkness.

When we landed in New York, I left the plane to phone the woman who was to have picked up the serval cubs in Texas. They had arrived safely, which relieved my mind. On returning to board, I found Morgan le Fey, who had been at Isis Oasis for the original convocation for the Fellowship of Isis. With her was Shasta, who had been at the Castle and carried on the work of the Fellowship for many years. We happily reacquainted ourselves and I introduced them to the other women in our group on the plane.

The eight of us were met by my sister Caryl at the Cairo airport. She had decided to join us after arranging to trade her home in Hawaii for a condo in Athens plus a house on a nearby island called Aegina. She was to be ordained in Egypt at the Temple of Hathor. Her husband had died recently and she wanted to reinvent herself, she said. A graduate of Stanford University, a teacher, and wife of a professor, she usually hung out with a more conservative crowd, but this was to be her time of initiation.

We were met by a travel guide who took us to the Mena House, which is the best place to stay in Cairo. Once there we snacked in the coffee shop and found our rooms to rest in after the long journey. Some of us found a path to view the Great Pyramid in night's blackness.

Day one was spent getting acquainted at breakfast, going to Gouda's shop called "The Tree of Life" at the foot of the Great Pyramid. Gouda was a friend from my previous visits to Egypt. We purchased perfumes and scarves and sniffed essential oils, one of which was named "Ioasis," after our center. Gouda had a picture of the Temple and our flyer stuck in a glass case and even an old write-up about his shop which mentioned Isis Oasis. He invited us to have dinner the next day and see the light show from his roof, where the view of the Sphinx and the Pyramids was particularly good. His family had lived there for hundreds of years and his brother, Ahmed, was a well-known as a guide for such groups as ours. It was a blessing to have this family taking care of us on this trip.

The Egyptian National Museum was our destination that day. We finally got going after the women had their first chance to bargain in a little shop in the village of Nazlet el Sammen. The museum was impressive and we hired an excellent guide who took us through in three hours. We visited the new mummy room, a well-designed space where visitors are asked to keep silent. Here the unwrapped bodies of the Pharaohs and Queens lay, including Ramses II, with his red hair still intact. It was a grim reminder of the tenuousness of all life. I was struck by the look of some of the mummies, who seemed lost in an ecstatic journey of endless time.

After viewing the boggling array of statuary and artifacts, we boarded a dinner cruise on the *Golden Pharaoh*, a beautifully decorated boat that, besides having delicious food, offered lively entertainment, including an amazing whirling dervish. We spent some time ogling the wonderful depictions of a whole pantheon of Gods and Goddesses that were portrayed on the curved ceiling of the upper deck. I envisioned a Quonset hut redone in like manner on the Isis Oasis grounds, and also a boat that would appear as though it were an Egyptian barge of ancient times.

The next day our driver, Abrahim, took us to Saquarra, past pastoral scenes to the Step Pyramid of Zoser. We spent a lot of the day roaming around the complex. In a nearby location we descended to the catacombs of the Apis bulls. This was quite a mystery and a most fantastic accomplishment of this culture, though its purpose is difficult to understand. We rode home amidst a lovely Egyptian sunset highlighting pyramids along the desert. We stopped at a rug-making school and witnessed young children whose delicate fingers maneuvered the rug designs most deftly. A controversy about children working was hotly discussed on our ride home.

Once back, we all got ready to go to Gouda's rooftop for the light show and dinner at his apartment, where we met his family. He seemed to be prospering and, judging from the respect shown him in the village, was thought of something akin to a Pharaoh. Returning to the Mena House, we prepared to get up early to enter the Great Pyramid the next day.

Miraculously, all Priestesses were ready on time to begin the difficult ascent within the Pyramid. A group of Japanese tourist followed us into the Queen's chamber, but soon we were left alone to engage in ritual. We remained in this feminine space for quite some time, chanting and meditating. Then we began the further ascent to the King's chamber. Three young Egyptian men appeared and sang for us, then joined with us in our Goddess songs and dances. They stayed to circle with us. Elizabeth did a beautiful temple dance with her usual grace and style and I sang my Isis song. Our voices rose in magnificence to the ceiling sending chills down spines. We ended by chanting "Let the Yin begin, let the Goddess in," and we closed our circle to descend onto the sands of the desert.

Shasta, Morgan, and Elizabeth went riding on Arabian horses through the desert and those of us with less stamina viewed the museum housing the Solar Boat next to the pyramid. Our guide was a man grown old while putting the boat together after it was found. He had a lot of class and at the initial part of the tour I asked if he wanted *baksheesh* (tip) for his guidance. He shook his head in the negative and said he was part of the museum. Still, at the end of the tour he said very politely, "You were right madam. I would like something for my work." I gave him a generous tip, well-earned and deserved. He seemed such an intrinsic part of the boat, pointing out photos showing him on the dig that uncovered the vessel that had remained in its sarcophagus until recently. Another boat had been found near this one and the Japanese were taking responsibility for the excavation and restoration.

Tired and hungry, we walked back to Gouda's shop, where we asked about a good place for lunch. "Right here!" said Gouda, and off he went to purchase delicious falafels and all the fixings. He gave me three boxes of Isis Herbal Tea as a gift as well. His lovely young daughters played happily nearby. His hospitality was overwhelming and there was nothing we could do to pay him back. *I will return his hospitality when he comes to California*, I thought.

Then to the desert once more to visit the Sphinx and discover the *mastabas* which surround the great Pyramids. Children were out of school because it was election day and we mingled with charming young girls on an outing as well as friendly youth who tested us on our knowledge of ancient Egypt and approved heartily when we passed.

When our shoes became sandy and our legs tired, we wandered back to Gouda's. Loud music began to play as we approached the enigmatic Sphinx, and a resonant man's voice speaking in Arabic came from a loud speaker. It sounded as though the Sphinx was talking. People gathered and we followed them to find ourselves face to face with the glorious monument while dramatic music played and a glowing sunset hovered over the pyramids.

A young man approached us with several sheets of painted papyrus. The one on top was Isis, which I offered to purchase for a dollar each in a lot of fifty or so. He accepted, and we all went to his shop for tea, while I picked out the proper papyrus.

Afterward he offered to drive us home, so we climbed into his vehicle, but he had not yet gotten in when it started to move backward down a hill filled with animals and children. I realized what was happening and an adrenaline rush reached my rather delicate heart, but we were saved by the ever-vigilant Egyptians, who stopped the car before anything bad happened. We got to our hotel in one piece.

This was our last night at the exotic Mena House, so we splurged a little at their posh restaurant where they had delightful entertainment. Carolyn especially enjoyed the folk dancing. Our flaming *crepes suzette*, lovingly prepared by an Egyptian chef, was shared by all.

The next morning we checked out. My sister wasn't feeling well, so we agreed to meet her later, after the rest of us went shopping in Kardesa, a little village of artisans near a picturesque canal. The best shop was way at the end in the back. Morgan and Shasta found it immediately and had an amazing amount of purchases stacked high. I bought a black and gold *abaya* and some scarves with glittery sparkles.

We were very happy with our treasures, and caught cabs back to the Mena House, where we got our luggage and left to board the airbus to Luxor. The flight was over before we knew it and I went looking for the man who was to pick us up. There was no one in the terminal and I became a bit concerned until we looked outside to find a man holding a sign depicting the Goddess Isis - my logo, in fact, and we knew we were being watched over.

Hany, our driver, was young, good-looking and well-educated. He loaded all our luggage on top of his car and off we went. During the stay at the Mena House we had made the arrangement to stay with him. We were shown three apartments, each on a different floor. We all chose the spaces that suited us best, sorted out our luggage and unpacked

B.J. did not like the apartment and pleaded with me to look for a villa for all of us. I told her that it would not be easy. She gloomily accompanied us to dinner with Hany and his cousin at a nearby restaurant, which we could never have found if we were not guided there. It was up a flight of stairs overlooking the teeming streets of the ancient city of Luxor, filled with amazing sights, sounds, smells and animal and vegetable life of all kinds. The meal was good and extremely inexpensive, but it took hours to serve, so we got back late, and fell into our hard, unfamiliar beds.

We had breakfast in the well-appointed apartment of Hany and his wife and baby, where three of our Priestesses were staying. Then we went off to the streets of Luxor to walk toward the temple. It was hard not to stop along the way to look and shop, so we designated a perimeter for intention so we could stay together.

It was a holiday and we saw many men were praying at a mosque. B.J. questioned a young man as to why only men were praying and we were invited into the mosque where we were shown a whole section for women in the balcony. The service was just ending. The women in their black attire regarded us in a manner that was cordial yet suspicious.

Our next adventure took us to the home of a young boy who met us on the street and insisted we stop in for tea. He proudly introduced us to his mother and sisters and a host of other women and children. We sat there wondering how to communicate with our hosts until I thought of singing. "Row, Row, Row Your Boat." That turned out to be a good ice-breaker, and all joined in with rowing motions and lots of smiles and vitality. Then Elizabeth got up to dance and the colorfully-clad women, each in a bright, almost Victorian-style house dress, danced and drummed on a wooden desk.

We all enjoyed the encounter and the hot tea refreshed us, but it was time to take our leave. One woman insisted we visit with her as well, so we had to decline and hastened on to walk toward the Luxor Temple. We strolled along the boardwalk to view the boats and the west bank of the Nile. There we spotted two villas overlooking the river, our dream villas, it seemed. B.J. marched up to the iron gate of the most elegant one and knocked upon the door. It didn't open.

A wise-looking old man in a *galabya* sat between the buildings, so we asked about the house. He told us the house was sleeping, but there was an office in the other house and he invited us to have a look. We went up the curved, broken marble steps flanked by ornate ironwork to a large room with tiled floors and pillars and a balcony with a divine view of the Nile and the west bank. The room was very dirty, with cigarette butts on the floor and dust in the corners, sorry neglect for so lovely a structure. B.J. announced her desire for a villa was cured.

We then tried to find our way to our apartments, but we couldn't quite, so we took a couple of carriages for only a few blocks before we were there. Our drivers overcharged us for our short ride.

Once settled, we gathered for a meeting. A talking pomegranate was put into service as each of us spoke our feelings. I talked about the changes that happen in Egypt and how lessons manifest quite quickly and warned that all would be touched by them. The pomegranate evoked other observations varying from the mundane to the profound.

Our host, Hany, helped us find spaghetti, as this is what we all had a taste for. The restaurant he took us to was really fancy, with a big buffet that was very delicious. We all over ate. Sophia kept us in stitches describing her fetish for fishes and the maître d' tried to make a date with her for a motorcycle ride.

When we left, I noticed that a large papyrus plant that was decorating the front of the restaurant had a broken stalk and asked one of the waiters to cut it for us. It was a great decoration for our living room. Its large triangular stalk barely fit into a water bottle and its enormous plumage brought a touch of the sacred to our simple decor. Night came, with the now familiar sounds of roosters, horses' hooves, the wheels of carts on the cobbled pavement, music and chanting from the mosques, ram's horns trumpeting, not to mention the sound of mating cats. We determined to get earplugs in the morning.

My sister Caryl had been up and down all night as she was suffering from "mummy tummy." This did not help me to sleep, but a shower in the morning got me moving. The bathroom was such that the water from the open shower went all over the floor and we had to use a squeegee to direct the bulk of it into a drain. It was not possible to enter without getting wet feet. The other facilities in the room were rather primitive also, but we learned in time to live with them.

Some of us went to Hany's apartment to have breakfast, which consisted of somewhat spicy beans, white rolls with jam, yogurt, and a hard boiled egg. Then we met again to arrange our itinerary. We were invited to lunch at the apartment of Hany's parents, who lived in the same building along with more of his family.

Hany's mother and father were a beautiful couple with wonderful smiles, inherited by their children. A large table was laden with food and all nine of us gathered around it. On the wall was a large painting of *The Last Supper*, as the family was Coptic Christian. There was a lot of meat in the food and many of us did not eat red meat. The tomato and lettuce salad had to be left as we were told that this was not safe food for foreigners who were not acclimatized to the local germs. But our conversation with the parents was as enlightening and endearing as it was touching to see how much these two loved each other and how they felt about their children. We discovered that they owned several buildings in the area and their children contributed by working, but jobs were not plentiful even though they had been well-educated. Most of the family in the building were doctors, including the father.

Later we ventured into the crowded market street to purchase some food to make a meal for all of us. We bought fruits of various kinds along with yogurt and honey and, after carefully washing and peeling them, we sat down to share this healthy repast.

A knock on the door brought us a surprise visitor: the gentleman from the Mena House who told us about these apartments. He came to see how we were doing and explained that Hany was worried that his English was not good enough and that his accommodations might not be suitable, so he was embarrassed to address us.

Martin Randall was a gregarious man and unabashedly joined in our conversation, which covered such unusual subjects as clitorectomies of young girls among the Arab population. He had a lot of information on the subject, as well as many suggestions about our stay, including tips like how to get on a luxury boat for very little money. Just then, Hany dropped in to tell us we could get a small boat with a cabin for each of us - a dream of mine. It was arranged for us to look at the boat the next day. We were expecting Amina, the tenth Priestess, a native of Luxor, to arrive that evening, but she never did.

The Goddess got me up early in the morning. I awoke to relieve myself and when I lay down again, I discovered a pen in my hand, surely a signal for me to arise again and write:

I think of Egypt as a symbol for the Goddess. Her land is barren save for the river flowing through, giving life and abundance to all along her banks. It is the land that supports us, nature that sustains us, the Goddess that we worship, Goddess of Nature. Nowhere is it more evident than here in this land, the cradle of civilization. There is much spirituality here still.

As I write, I hear the church bells calling those of Coptic Christian faith to prayer. Some of the Priestesses are going off to experience this today with the family we are living with. We have seen the men worshipping at the mosque in large numbers daily and found that women also have their place within, even though it is relegated to a small balcony. But we are here to immerse ourselves in the past and get in touch with the ancient ones and how they worshipped in their day at the once magnificent temples along the Nile.

The splendor of that time is so beyond what we are seeing today and the lives of the people were so much more refined.

We know this by their art, their architecture and the wisdom that they left behind in their hieroglyphic writings. How have we become so crude after so much refinement existed? If we consider a culture from a higher perspective, perhaps the Goddess was in her youth, glorious, beautiful and full of life. Glowing with vitality and then slowly crumbling, becoming corrupt, her supreme beauty fading as the twilight of time overtakes civilization and she dies out slowly, slowly.

And now, there are some of us struggling to rebirth the Goddess. To find those things that are still valuable left on the planet. Trying to discover what is real and useful...to make our lives enriched once again. To revive the old which was in reality the youth of civilization.

As Priestesses we must hold a vision of beauty and truth and spread this vision throughout the world. Starting from this place, Egypt, the source of life, is most appropriate.

By our action let us spread that aspect of light around the planet. Let us do this with joy and grace and delight in the process, for it need not be severe and dogmatic, but let us instead help others to rejoice in the love and energy of the Goddess.

At noon on Sunday we went to view the boat we might sail on. It had ten tiny cabins, one for each of us, a simple deck with mats on the floor and low metal tables, and only two bathrooms that looked a little rough. As we left via the rickety ramp, a group was boarding a somewhat larger boat, and the English woman in charge of this entourage said she really enjoyed her trips on these boats, but would not divulge the cost, having some loyalty to the crew. They asked us $48 per night per person. When we asked to see the kitchen, they said it was locked. We looked at the kitchen of the other boat and saw young male cooks stirring pots of zucchini and potatoes, which seemed plain but not unhealthy.

We opted to take a look at a luxury tourist boat, just picking one at random that was getting ready to sail. We were taken on a tour by the boat manager and witnessed the clean, air-conditioned cabins with baths, multiple floors with lounges furnished with plush chairs and ornate tables, and a deck with lots of lounge chairs and a pool and hot tub. We were invited to see the dining room where an opulent lunch was laid out consisting of many dishes in a lavish buffet display. The manager told us that they would sail the next day and because they were not full we could have our own rooms and all the amenities for $50 each. We left the glamorous vessel feeling confused.

The Winter Palace was our next destination, so there we would discuss this possibility and have lunch. We were wishing Amina would show up, as we were worried that we had not heard from her, when lo and behold, she magically appeared, dressed as I had remembered her, not in Egyptian garb but in an Indian pants suit, her tall gaunt figure looking a bit out of place. She had tracked us to this spot, and forthwith began to fill us in on what we needed to know relative to the deal with the boatman. She said private boats were generally higher priced and that we could try to control our food and water if we made the right arrangements. We had till 4 o'clock to make our commitment to the small boat.

This time we used a talking lemon. It was an interesting process to witness nine American Priestesses choose between opulence or total adventure with no amenities but more chance of the trip being a spiritual experience. The thought of comfort in a plush lounge chair while viewing the Nile was a great consideration. We decided we would all prefer to be alone on the small boat, but it needed to be cheaper and the kitchen needed to be inspected. Amina, B.J. and Morgan went to see the skipper. When they returned they had an agreement to have plenty of bottled water, good vegetarian food, freshly purchased, and the ability to visit the kitchen anytime, all for the price of $30 per person, which was as high as we had decided we would go.

Our trip now planned, we once again walked through the teeming streets, stopped by every merchant along the way, to rest in our apartment. Hany had offered to make calling cards for everyone and I had decided to have mine printed with the announcement of a new Lyceum to be launched at Isis Oasis upon my return. Soon, weariness overtook me and I slithered into bed exhausted and satisfied that all was going so well. We would sail day after tomorrow for five days.

The next morning was spent seeking *sistrums* (an ancient musical rattle) until it was time to visit the Temple of Luxor. We paraded through it in

---

silence, finding fascinating hieroglyphs and feeling the energy. We met with Amina and sat among the ruins while we shared and listened to each other. We walked through the temple again lit up under the moon, then went home to pack.

Tuesday morning found us all loaded down with Egyptian overnight bags, boarding the rickety plank of the boat of our choice, the *Domo 2*, The cabins had numbers on the doors, odd on one side and even on the other, and baths down the hall. It reminded me of the Lodge at Isis Oasis, except the narrow carpeted hallway was very uneven and indicated the condition of the boat was not the best. Each of us chose a cabin and met up on deck for breakfast of the usual beans and pita bread we had now become accustomed to. Soon the boat left the quay and we were gliding along the Nile. On such a small boat it was easy to see both banks simultaneously. It was so delicious, all of us on this antiquated, unassuming boat, gliding along the mighty Nile River…a wish come to fruition.

I went to a seat in the center of the rear deck. Closing my eyes I could visualize my ancient journey, the one I had seen in a past life session. I viewed myself in jeweled sandals and wondered where I am going. In another past life session I found myself again on the boat and this time I knew I was going to a special festival in my honor. Strangely, I also knew I never arrived at my destination. In this life I know I shall.

That night the boat would run late so we could

get to Philae by the next day for a full moon ritual in the evening. We sailed past picturesque scenes while eating tasty and healthy meals that were served to us. The moonrise and sunset simultaneously displayed for us while we sang and studied and spoke of the *neters* of ancient Egypt, retelling the myth of Isis and Osiris. We worked with the Laws of Maat and got further through discussion and consensus to revise them and update them to meet the needs of our age in a positive way. Finally, we decided to go to bed in order to get up for the sunrise. The boat docked at Edfu for the night and would sail again at six, we were told. We would have another day of this river bliss before embarking for our private ceremony at Philae. So mote it be.

I rose to see the sunrise and Morgan did the same. It was cold on the deck and we wondered if warmth would come soon with the sun. Together we witnessed a glorious sight as golds, pinks and orchids filled the sky from the black of night. Then a turquoise blue evolved as a linear flock of birds passed through the beauteous image. The Nile reflected all this wonder graciously into its ever-flowing sacred waters. A lotus plant floated by and two kites skimmed the river as the sky became ever brighter. Then the sun, in all its glory, began its ascent as it has for millions of years. Its glowing presence filled us with the same awe and reverence that has filled all sun worshippers who preceded us, and we raised our arms, palms out toward the sun, and chanted the name of Ra.

Breakfast and a nice cup of hot tea awaited us. The afternoon went by with various activities, such as creating Neter Yoga, practicing our new song, "I like to smile when I see the Nile," and working on the 42 Laws of Maat.

Soon the skipper announced that we would get to the island of Philae very shortly, so we hastened to don our white garbs that we had decided was the proper way to visit the Temple of Isis. We were all very grateful to our boatmen for the sensitivity to our desires and the way they strove to get us there on time.

When we were all ready, we had to disembark on a narrow plank onto a very precarious pile of stones. We then had to traverse a thin ledge on a high stone wall until we could jump down into a field full of broken glass and horse dung. A cab was waiting to drive us through the streets of Aswan and we got a boat to the temple, across the beautiful bay with mounds of stones rising from the waters. Once upon the island, we found the wondrous temple still vacant of tourists. We joined in a circle around the central altar under the full moon in the courtyard of the Holy of Holies. Our ritual was very powerful. We left a sprig of basil as an offering. Returning to the boat was a little scary, but we had flashlights to get across the field and the stone wall, then mount the gangplank that was so rickety and tippy.

Five of us decided to return to the temple at sunrise. I was ready to go at 5:30 as were Caite, Carolyn, Morgen, and Elizabeth. We had told our driver to pick us up at 6 o'clock, but realized that would not get us to the Temple on time to observe sunrise on the water. This caused a bit of anxiety until we looked across the field and discovered our driver was there waiting for us, half an hour early, seeming to have understood our need. We disembarked once again via that incredibly rickety plank and clambered over the stones, then walked the thin ledge of the wall and finally dropped to the garbage-laden field, moving cautiously to the awaiting taxi.

There was no one on the streets as we sped toward our destination. The familiar sign showing Philae Temple loomed up and soon we were at the boat dock, but all was deserted. As we stepped out of the taxi, dogs began to bark from all directions. *Anubis is here to guide us,* I thought, *and all will be well.* The ornate iron gate with the lotus decoration opened for us and soon we saw, high on a hill, an old man in a pale green *galabya*. He appeared out of a temple-like house with brilliant blue shutters. Surveying the situation, he descended the hillside on a serpentine road. He understood what we wanted and set about to get his boat ready to take us through the magical waters, still in moonlight and shrouded in mist.

We climbed into the boat, which glided over the water past the temple gates. We gestured to the boatman to go first to the sacred spot from where the original Temple of Isis had stood before it was moved to its present site because of the Aswan dam. It felt so mystical as the boatman tied up his boat where huge boulders jutted up silhouetted against the sky, which was growing lighter. He helped us with loving eyes and sturdy hands to climb the boulders. There was sincere understanding in his noble regal face. We all stood together facing the east where the sun would rise and the day coming forth would begin. Soon we took off again with the aid of the caring boatman and headed to the new temple site. The old boatman went off to secure tickets for us and arrange that we enter the temple earlier than normal. This was only agreed to after we danced on the deck to the guard's amazement. He simply could not refuse us, and so we had the temple to ourselves on this glorious morning.

We headed for the Holy of Holies in procession. The basil from the night before was still on the altar. We added our crystals and sacred objects, incense and a candle. We all placed our hands on the black granite altar, chanting and incanting, when suddenly a kite, the bird associated with Isis, flew swiftly in our direction. We all saw this as a sign that Isis was with us.

Suddenly the chamber lit up and tourists began coming in our direction. We knew that we had reactivated the Holy of Holies in the Temple of Isis for all time with our devotions last night under the full moon and this morning in the new sunrise of day, with five of us adding a spark of life to the slowly decaying temple.

Returning once more to our boat, we had our

usual bean breakfast before we took off on a shopping spree in Aswan. Later we sailed around the island of Elephantine and found the mythical source of the Nile. We gave up our old uncomfortable habits as we each threw a gift into the waters and prayed for that which would fulfill us anew. I gave up the day-to-day mundane at Isis Oasis and filled it with a Lyceum.

On the way back we stopped at the Old Cataract Hotel and discovered they made great ice cream sundaes. A lively band played on the stage and one of the musicians gave Carolyn a tip about what kind of drum to buy and where to get it. We went back to our boat home amid the magical lights of Aswan sparkling with exotic design in the waters of the Nile.

Morning came and we sailed to Kom Ombo. We waited until the tourist boats had gone, then disembarked and walked past fields with white donkeys who let us pet them.

We walked in silence to the rear of the Temple and descended into the tunnel, one by one, to experience an intense feeling of death and rebirth. In this state we wandered through the temple. Exquisite bas-reliefs revealed their secrets only slightly as we found *neters* (goddesses and gods) we were attracted to. While we roamed about I noticed my sister Caryl was crying and I embraced her to comfort her. The experience of the underground was powerful to all of us in different ways. It was good for her to let go and have a cleansing cry. We all discovered a series of fascinating birthing scenes and the mummified crocodiles left us in an altered state.

We walked back past the vendors, stopping to buy a few more treasures. A group of young men and women were coming towards us from a boat, beating drums. We danced a bit with them as we met on the path and one took Carolyn's finger cymbals, which she gave up graciously.

When we boarded our boat again, lunch was waiting. Caite presided over a writing workshop and we read our offerings. Dinner came next and we made it a point to thank the crew for cooking in a style that befitted us. Our dinner conversation centered around stories of Clonegal Castle and Olivia, mostly told in a lively manner by Morgan and Shasta.

The day ended with a beautiful sunset, a harvest moon, and a band put together by the combined crew of the boats, *Domo 1* and 2, which were moored together. They sang and danced, and we were all delighted at this burst of frivolity.

Earlier I had visualized a band on board playing for us, but I had not quite imagined it might be the crew. As I climbed, exhausted, into my bunk bed, I wondered about visualization. So many times in my life I had envisioned something that came true if I held the thought, or if I would draw or write down what I imagined would happen, often enough, it would! Magic!

The town of Edfu awaited us in the morning and we kept our eyes straight ahead so the merchants would not detain us with their beseeching. Huge statues of god Horus greeted us as we headed for the Holy of Holies of his ancient temple. We had waited till the other boats had gone so we could be alone there. We made our offerings at the altar, then each of us climbed into the black granite box which once housed the main idol. We thus became Horus, each in our own way, and prayed for that which is good, for peace in the world, for universal kindness.

We inspected the wonders carved on every inch of stone and finally departed the temple to go through the avenue of vendors once more. We purchased a gift for the boatmen that had taken such good care of us, a stone head of Hatshepsut for their masthead.

Some of us returned to the boat, but our carriage, which included Amina, went off in search of a pastry shop to buy special treats for the celebration of our last night on the boat. We found the place that Amina was searching for and while she shopped, we lingered outside, drinking in the exotic scene.

The streets were rutted and muddy but it was fascinating to watch the daily life going by. I gave a pencil to a dimpled child and spoke with some curious and polite schoolgirls as they passed. Men in pastel and earthy *galabayas* walked purposefully to and fro and a herd of goats paraded by. The *calleche* (carriage) took an easier way back than we had come, thank goodness, as it had almost overturned in the search for pastries.

Back on the boat, I wrote in my journal. Some of us had become ill along the way and I suddenly felt nauseous at the first bite of dinner. I had enough energy to present the crew their gifts which, besides the head of Hatshepsut, included a colorful scarf that we thought would look nice hanging along the back corridor of the row of cabins. Then I retired to my cabin to rest. The boat docked for the evening near a small island.

In the morning we sailed to Esna. I was feeling better. We hired two taxis for our adventures to the temple with its great pillars of the magnificent Hypostyle Hall. We made our way down a long stairway, as the temple had been buried and the town of Esna had grown up, around and over it. The colors were quite evident on the temple walls. It contained some unusual and startling figures, blending the flowing late Romanesque and Egyptian styles.

Hany and his driver had come to pick us up in Esna but could not find us, so we took the taxis back to our apartment. It was starting to feel like home, this bright, noisy street. Hany passed out the cards he had made for us. Some were not accurate and even if we only ordered black with gold printing, Hany had chosen to make them multiple colors. I was happy to have Lyceum cards made in Egypt and felt it would prove fortuitous.

We were exhausted and hungry and went to El Dar for lunch. I ate delicately and then fell into bed where I slept without stirring for thirteen hours. During this sleep I had a dream that was very strange so I wrote it down to ponder. Dreams can be so mysterious and I am certain they often portend something most important, but it is difficult in the waking state to know what the meaning might be. By writing it down you can put the material on the back burner until you discover whether it may be oracular in nature.

We intended to spend our afternoon at the Winter Palace, so we started the day by cooking a nice omelet on our stove. Everything took so long in Egypt, as there were virtually no conveniences, but we made do in many and variable ways. I had imagined being in the garden of the Winter Palace all day, but we were delayed, for once everyone was done faxing and banking we ended up only being able to have tea in the drawing room. We gathered around a round table in the very center of the drawing room and worked on the Laws of Maat rather animatedly. Others in the room were looking at us somewhat in dismay, as I suspect we were being more lively than is expected in a tea room atmosphere.

Some went home after tea and others stayed for dinner. We were not admitted to the grand dining room as they said it was reservation only and booked that evening. We repaired to the coffee shop where I had the thinnest filet of sole I could ever have imagined being served anywhere, and why they called it a filet is beyond my imagination since it consisted entirely of bones.

It is sometimes difficult to stay well while visiting Egypt, and when morning came we met together with the exception of Carolyn and Shasta, who were ill. We, the unafflicted, headed for the tourist ferry to cross the Nile and visit the Temple of Queen Hatshepsut, four tombs in the Valley of Kings, and Nefertari's Tomb, which was supremely divine, having been beautifully restored. Then we spent the evening with Amina's adopted family, seeing the sunset from their roof and chanting.

We discovered the best restaurant that we had yet experienced, which had authentic Egyptian food done with a flair. The rest of the evening we spent with carvers of alabaster in their apartment, watching them work and smoking a little hashish with them. It was a surprising finale to the day but we had a good time and felt a little naughty.

The Habu Rest House offered us a chance to sleep on the West Bank in the quiet of Mertsager, Goddess of silence. The hashish afforded me a deep sleep, but I awoke to see the sunrise. By opening the back door and stepping out on the verandah, one could see beyond verdant green fields to the Nile. Pink clouds hovered profusely in a lavender and turquoise sky. I played a tape of beautiful soothing music and Caryl joined me in watching the scenery. A few men rode by on bicycles and a few children passed and then a pack of dogs played and cavorted in this otherwise peaceful scene. The other side of the vaulted room had another set of double doors that opened to the Madinet Habu Temple.

We enjoyed breakfast on the verandah (after

getting past the flushless toilets) and soon we were off again to visit the Ramuseum and the Tombs of the Nobles, which showed scenes of daily life, rich in hunting, fishing, wine-making, music and dance. Lunch was a duplicate of last night's dinner, as we really wanted an encore of our delicious feast of the previous evening. All agreed, you could never have too much of a good thing.

Soon we had only a short time to see Medinet Habu Temple. There were a lot of cars on the road and we heard there was a dignitary in town. It turned out that Mabarak, Egypt's president, was at the temple and we watched as he exited with his entourage, like an ancient pharaoh. Amina got to shake his hand and later appeared on television, making her more popular with her friends in Luxor. We had only a short time to see Medinet Habu Temple, so I decided to return to the West Bank, but not to stay another night at the Habu Rest House. Our apartment, by comparison, was much more palatable. Elizabeth chose to stay on and later told us of her experiences visiting a monastery of nuns. We took the people's ferry this time, and were objects of animated attention during the short ride.

I called home and Paul told me we had a newborn ocelot. I slept late, dreaming of ocelots, and we spent the balance of the day shopping for food and cooking spaghetti. When Amina came by, I bought vests for the Isis crew at home, spices, scarves, and I studied some papyrus trying to choose what might be good to sell in the little shop at Isis Oasis. We visited a neighbor who had a television, hoping to see the news showing Amina shaking hands with President Mubarak, but it had been on the night before. Although we were a little disappointed, it was interesting to spend some time in this typically Arabic household.

On awakening we set off to shop once again. I had to exchange some of the vests which seemed the wrong size when I examined them. I also went to a shop across from our apartment to order fifty papyrus paintings. First we had to have the traditional tea with the owner, Ali, before we discussed changing a Maat depiction to Isis by putting a different headdress on her. We discussed colors I would like. I gave him a rather hefty deposit when he agreed he could do this.

In the afternoon we assembled for another visit to Karnak. This time we found the large statue of Sekhmet in a tiny chapel lit by an opening in the ceiling. We stayed in this space observing the powerful image as the light shone on it in its total perfection. We touched her, hugged her, growled with her, and asked for her strength to guide us in our future trials. When the guards beckoned for us to leave, we climbed some ancient steps nearby to find a sunset with a rainbow in the sky. A giant girder for temple repair looked so strange along side of Hatshepsut's obelisk. It seemed a symbol for bridging the present with the past.

The Hilton Hotel was our destination for dinner and a fabulous spread was available there. We took a people's taxi back to our place at the meager cost of 25 *piasters* and soon we were home, earplugs firmly in place, to sleep.

After a slow start the next day a number of us got in two *calleches* and journeyed through the back streets to the Hotel Jolie Vie on Crocodile Island. It was a divine hotel in a lush setting on the Nile. We dined on really good food at not overly expensive prices. The staff was pleasant, unlike the Winter Palace, and a large pink pelican visited our table, a pet of the place. After lunch we discovered there was a zoo and we visited crocodiles, peacocks and other birds, monkeys, donkeys, camels, goats and sheep plus a pond of ducks that reminded me of home. They had a wonderful vegetable garden, very fertile, and a garden of many colored roses, some of which we snipped to take with us. We got back to our waiting *calleches* and galloped through the interesting maze of streets with never-ending images full of wonder.

That evening we purchased food to take with us on our journey to Dendera. We had to figure out if we could also go to Abydos or not. We were getting reports that were negative, but we fantasized that we might go disguised as wailing Arabic women in black garb on our way to a funeral. Then the final word came from Hany, who said the tourist police said no go. The temple was off limits due to terrorism.

So, in the morning, after the traditional Egyptian breakfast of beans, eggs, and fresh pita bread, we donned our goddess clothes and boarded a mini bus with a very respectful driver who did not speak much English. Our journey was long, through incredibly beautiful terrain mixed with little industrial villages along a canal.

Eventually Dendera came into view. We were adopted by a pleasant tourist policeman who began to show us how Horus was suckled by Hathor using his fingers to demonstrate a baby getting milk from a teat. We asked if he could take us to a quiet place for ceremony and he guided us to a small Isis Temple behind the huge edifice.

The main chamber had a large scaffolding in it, so we selected a narrow hall which was probably a robing room. Caryl was to be ordained here, so we set up an altar on a bale of straw seemingly put there for this purpose. I had brought a yellow rose to use in the ritual and later photos told me this was just the right thing. Caryl conducted herself well, accepting her new role with dignity and grace, then bestowing her first blessing.

The Temple was awesome. We went into the underground passageway and found symbols and baffling, strange figures beyond our immediate comprehension. We knew that here the secrets were stored. Our minds were reeling as we exited with what we had seen and experienced in this birthing Temple of Hathor.

We collected more than usual *backsheesh*, but we thought our very special guide was worth it.

We had lunch in a little park nearby where young urchins came to beg. We bought cold drinks gratefully from one of them and we shared some of our lunch with each, including an old women who sat on her haunches nearby.

Once home, we made dinner with rice and veggies and lentil soup, another staple of Egypt. We ended the day with a myriad of subjects, like how we all need a circle of friends and our role as Priestesses is to open ourselves to this and to working with others on the principles of the Laws of Maat. By now we had recreated all forty-two of them, turning them into perfect messages for the present day in a positive way. We had done this as a group project, which was important to give focus and content to our being together.

With only a few days left, Caryl and I jumped into a *callesh* with Hassan, a young boy who had been helping us purchase things and go places. He suggested the Camel Market. We traveled through the outskirts of Luxor, seeing parts of the city new to us. Each image was a picture that stayed in our minds. People waived at us constantly and little children ran along side begging pencils. When we reached the Camel Market, all the camels had been sold, so we chalked the experience up to seeing the countryside and watched two men struggling with their new cow, which looked just like a picture out of a tomb.

Our next adventure took us to the Sheridan Hotel where we had lunch on the terrace and then made our way back home. Hany was coming back from Cairo and we were invited to celebrate his birthday at his apartment. He had brought wonderful pastries from the city and we supplied ice cream, but found out the family was fasting at this time and could not eat with us. Hany got out some drums and told us he had wanted to be a musician but his father, a well-respected doctor, forbade it. Magna, Hany's beautiful and talented sister, also played drums and showed Carolyn the beats to play Arabic music.

We arranged to take Hany to a nightclub along with his wife, his nephew, his cousin, and a host of us. We went to a swinging, swank little disco in the Gaddis Hotel, where all was decorated like a temple with humorous Tut faces on pillars and waiters in Tut headdresses. We all danced wildly on the small dance floor, especially Caryl, who found an Egyptian escort who tied a scarf around her and gave her quite a whirl. Hany and his wife did not dance, however, and we learned that after marriage few Egyptian men dance with their wives. His relative, a psychiatrist, said because of this he would prefer dancing to marriage. Rafik, another relative who was studying to be a guide, also liked to dance and graciously took a number of us on, dancing with two women at a time. We got home late, knowing that we wanted an early start, as we planned to revisit the West Bank, the Temple of Medinet Habu, and some more tombs. Rafik would accompany us.

When morning came, I went over to see if the papyrus I had ordered were in. They were not, so I started to get a little worried.

Rafik, Carolyn, Caite, B.J. and I had a fascinating walk through the Medinet Habu Temple. We discovered the chapels of the Votrises, powerful priestesses who ruled during certain periods. This was the most compelling aspect to us and it was nice to have Rafik with us to help us as we went. No *baksheesh* was required when we had an Egyptian with us, it seemed. The Queen's and the children's tombs were a profound experience. We returned home aboard the tourist ferry after waiting for quite awhile. Once again I checked on the papyrus I had ordered, and once again it was not ready. Most of us went off to the Isis Hotel for dinner, where we dined on Chinese food made by a Pakistani chef. We cased the hotel and shopped without buying and finally returned home, I checked again on the papyrus, but they were not there. Would I ever get them?

We visited a girls' school for commercial studies where girls were typing with one finger in a beginning class. We passed out pencils to a horde of beautiful, young, vibrant girls and met the principal of this dilapidated school. There was a large hole in the roof over a planter box filled with dusty, dying plants. Dirt and broken windows were everywhere. When we left, the principle invited us to visit his bazaar. Even teachers needed a subsidy beyond their salary.

We then visited some papyrus workshops.

The pieces were immense and rather fancy and the prices were high, but the work was excellent. Ali, at the papyrus shop opposite our apartment, had failed to get me what I wanted and I managed to get my deposit back. Amina advised me to tell Ashroff, her vendor friend, to get me some papyrus. He asked me for some money and said he would see me later.

We were to gather at our apartment to leave for Crocodile Island in a *falucca*, a colorful wooden sailboat commonly used for transportation up and down the Nile. Hassan had arranged for a boat to be waiting. Our time was short as the *falucca* would not sail at night. Morgan and Shasta were missing, but finally showed up at the wharf where we were waiting. There was no wind and we had to be towed for a ways.

We arrived at last at the Jolie Vie Hotel where, due to the time of day, we were limited to cold sandwiches. The pet pelican showed up as before. There was no time for dessert, as the sun was setting over the Nile and it was very quickly getting darker.

We boarded the *falucca* once again. This time they let out the forty-foot sails and we quietly glided toward Luxor Temple in the fading sunset. We clambered up the steps to enter the Temple for a ceremony for the Winter Solstice. We walked down the Avenue of the Rams and back again in silence, meeting in the central temple of Hatchepsut. Here we gathered around a granite altar to invoke the goddesses we knew and ones we had recently met. We called for Hatshepsut to be with us, then we walked to the end of the Temple. In a small courtyard between pillars we did the Raising of the Djed Ceremony while respectful guards watched from a distance. No tourists interfered and we had the space to ourselves as we wished. It was a good and fitting way to end the journey of the Nine Priestesses. We strolled home through the crowded streets to rest one last time at our adopted home.

In the morning Hassan came by and sold me a pair of pajamas for Paul. I went to see Ashroff and purchased a bunch of Isis and Maat papyrus. I gave a small Maat papyrus to everyone, along with the copies of the forty-two Virtuous Laws of Maat that we had reworded. Everyone was trying to do everything at once and saying goodbye was difficult. After much complication, Hany found the proper airport to go to Cairo, connecting to Athens.

It was time to say farewell to Egypt once again, but I likely shall return as I have done three times before. Always it is a treasure and a joyous journey of discovery.

Athens was such a change from Egypt. An elegant apartment awaited us, tastefully decorated with a modern black and white decor. We wandered around Athens a few days, discovering ancient artifacts, pastry shops, *tavernas* and museums. We spent Christmas in Athens, then made our way to the island of Aegina, where we stayed in a house made of stone which had been an olive press until it was remodeled by the present owners. In the living room were all the remnants of the olive oil workings: a giant stone for grinding the olives, a trough, a large metal press and a kind of stone kiln for further extracting oil.

The most amazing thing about this room was the subterranean viewing mound, complete with light that would allow us to see down into the very womb of the Earth. The woman of the house was a Goddess person and taught women's studies at various universities. It was most wonderful to stay in this historic structure which had kept so much of its authenticity. There were four cats also to amuse us with their charming antics.

A car came with the place and we used it to ferry to the Peloponnese and visit sites and villages that sprang up in the midst of orange groves and olive trees. We spent the morning of New Year's Day on the top of a high hill on which a ruined fortress was perched, overlooking the wondrous expanse of land. It brought to mind the ancient Greek myths that I have always so loved.

Our journey took us to other islands like Poros and Idra and the places we stayed at were always overlooking the sea. It was a time to reflect and rest and soon I began to ruminate on my return home.

What would greet me? How could I make things better? Where would I put my energies? What direction would Isis Oasis take? My sister, who was recovering from losing he husband, would stay on in Greece three months more after I had left, all by herself, knowing few people. I thought she was very brave to do this and to commit to the idea that she might begin to reinvent herself at this time. I left after two weeks in Greece. The arduous airplane ride back took me to Egypt once again, but only at the airport, where I connected with a plane that would take me home.

Being high in the air always inspires me to dream of new possibilities and ideas. It is while in the stratosphere that I thought of doing a play on Hatshepsut, the female pharaoh that ruled in peace for twenty two years and took her architect as a lover. He built her mortuary temple that is one of the wonders of the world. I thought of it as being a narrative with song and dance on seven locations on the grounds of Isis Oasis, and this indeed came about. I did the narration while a number of the priestesses and priests took part. Elizabeth, the beautiful dancer played Hatshepsut, and Diveena sang the seven songs I wrote for it. I was gratified that I heard a women in the audience say it was the best play she ever saw. We performed it several more time after that.

The thought of a tomb room came to me during this flight from the land of Egypt. I had so loved being in the tombs of the kings, queens, and nobles that I wished to reproduce the feeling I had while being in their midst.

There was a space under the theatre that would make a perfect tomb room. It had stone steps leading to a concrete floor and was about twelve feet square. I could paint the walls with scenes from the actual tombs and embellish it with hieroglyphs. I could have a sarcophagus built and people could lie in it. There could be music inserted into the mattress of the box to give a feeling of timelessness, and inspire a journey to the most sacred places of the soul.

When I returned I had such a box built. It had the protective Goddesses, Isis, Nepthys, Selket, and Neith on each corner and a large scarab placed on top to complete the effect. The walls became painted with the boat of a million years and the scene of the weighing of the heart on the scales of Maat.

We offered a weekend for women who could stay in a private room, have a massage, a tarot reading with an Egyptian deck, and an hour in the tomb room. In addition they could tour the animals and birds and attend our Sunday ceremony in the Grand Temple. This, indeed, was the beginning of the Lyceum of Isis Oasis.

I conceived of month long trainings where young potential priestesses could visit and have the opportunity to spend a month in our sanctuary, but as of yet, this has not materialized.

In this modern era it would have to be weekends only. The ancient Egyptians, I had learned, spent three months out of the year in the temples along the Nile.

As the plane touched ground in San Francisco, I was already anxious to get started on my new projects.

At the Mena House upon arrival in Egypt

Nine Priestesses at the Temple of Hathor at Dendara

Nine Priestesses at the Hotel Jolie Vie

Loreon ordaining her sister, Caryl, at the Temple of Isis

Loreon contemplating the 42 Ideals of Maat

Carolyn and Loreon dancing for the guards at the Isis Temple at Philae

CHAPTER XI

The ANIMALS and BIRDS WHO LIVE at ISIS OASIS

*P*aul was there to greet me as I got off the plane. He looked so different from the Paul that I remembered greeting me after my first trip to Egypt fifteen years ago. I remembered that he had looked quite handsome and full of energy as he held the bunch of flowers for me at that time. Now he was leaning on a cane, barely able to walk. We both collapsed in the purple house on Folsom Street where I have continued to find much solace after being in the midst of turmoil at Isis Oasis. Here in the city things were always the same, as though I had never left. After a good night's sleep, we headed north back to Geyserville.

I was eager to meet baby Ramses, the latest addition to our ocelot family, offspring of Pharaoh and Sheba, grandson to Karma and Milo, who had been offspring of Caesar and Trilby whom I had as pets thirty-five years ago right here in San Francisco. The family just keeps going and growing.

Things had stayed pretty together at Isis Oasis in my absence, and for all of this I was thankful, especially considering the raging storms battering Northern California. The Egyptian geese that I had worried about upon leaving did, indeed, disappear, but a wonderful waterfall had been created to replaced the culvert that had always ruined the look of the pond. I was most especially thankful to those who lived there and took care of the baby ocelot, getting up all hours of the night to bottle feed him.

Several months passed and I was arranging one day to pick up a new pair of Egyptian geese when Nick, who had built the waterfall, pulled up with an impish smile on his face. "Look inside the van," he said. There were the two Egyptian geese that had taken off. The very ones that were responsible for my broken ankle and who had mocked me as I left for Egypt, Nick had seen them on a road north of Geyserville, just walking down the highway. He had managed, albeit not without a great deal of difficulty, to capture them.

It seemed like a magical happening fraught with meaning. Paul said anything that is truly yours cannot be lost. I felt responsible to pick up the birds that I had ordered anyway, and so we ended up with four Egyptian geese, a breed which is now extinct in Egypt. Perhaps that is the meaning: as we connect more and more with that ancient culture here, we are resurrecting the very symbology of the Old Kingdom, where love, beauty and abundance once flourished along the Nile. We will not let all that wisdom die and thereby shall keep alive the ancient Goddesses and Gods so they may be acknowledged in this new age.

Shortly after the Wild Egyptian Goose Chase, my golden pheasant died. On that very day, a neighbor called to say there was a red and gold bird in their tree and had I lost one? Of course, I said yes, not explaining how I had lost mine. I sent a few guys on the staff to look for it, but it had flown off. Then another neighbor called about the same thing. The identical scenario happened and no bird was found. At the end of the day, the grammar school called and said this red and gold bird was on the roof of their school, This time, the two young men on the staff were successful at catching the bird and it was a golden peasant just like the one that had died. This one was very friendly and responded to commands. He would always jump up on a perch when I told him to and he seemed to love people. Isis certainly took care of me on that day, providing Isis Oasis another wonderful golden pheasant. These are from China and not indigenous to our area.

We have quite a collection of beautiful pheasants at Isis Oasis for they are always such a pleasure for the guests to see in their myriad of designs and colors. Besides the golden pheasant, whose head feathers look like the headdresses of the pharaohs of ancient Egypt in orange and black stripes, we have the Amhearst pheasant, with similar headdress but in different colors. The two kinds always elicit *oohs* and *ahs* from those who visit them. We also have grey peacock pheasants, which have many spots that change from a shimmering purple to turquoise, depending on which way they are facing when the sun hits them. We have the Temmenicks tragopan, also spotted, with the male having an amazing blue color around the eyes, and the Impyan pheasant, with its scintillating blue and copper colors. There is the Mongolian ringneck, with purple and gold feathers and a white collar; the silver pheasant, looking like its going to an elegant black and white ball; and the Palawan pheasant, with its amazing turquoise body and large purple spotted tail feathers.

Many birds were given to us because they needed homes when their owners can no longer take care of them, and we built aviaries for them opposite our giant Douglas fir tree. We were given a pair of lavender crowned parrots, a blue front parrot, and a red lored parrot named Charlie. Charlie is quite a character, having lived with a rather cantankerous old lady for fifteen years. His vocabulary includes lots of swearing, which he mutters under his breath.

We were also given a beautiful white cockatoo named Sydney, who says "Hello!" to everyone; a blue and gold macaw who is very friendly; and a hybrid macaw we call Ixchel, after the Mayan Rainbow Goddess. Ixchel is the most beautifully colored macaw you will ever see. I could hardly believe I was given this bird, as I saw one similar in Costa Rica at a bird sanctuary and fell in love with it. The combination of two kinds of macaws does not happen in the wild but only in captivity.

We also have many cockatiels and parakeets, along with some unusual birds like the plumhead and a rare Barnard parakeet we have not yet been able to find a mate for.

One day our male Indian ringneck escaped from his aviary during a weekend when we had a concert and the musicians opened the safety door and unknowingly let him out. We watched helplessly as he flew away. Shortly afterward, I got a call from a women I know who has many birds. The bird rescue of Santa Rosa had called her about a bird that matched the description of the one I had lost. It was a male Indian ringneck, just like the one that flew away, but it was not ours. We took it home anyway, and now they have made new babies. Being that both parents are green, we were surprised that one of the chicks was pure yellow.

We have many doves, both ringneck and pure white, and fancy fantail pigeons that fly around in the habitats of the pheasants. Our peacocks never fail to be wonderful models for our guests' cameras. We have both blue and white ones that offer us their fabulous feathers every year as they molt, giving us wonderful decorations for our rooms.

The pond holds some ducks along with our Egyptian geese and black and white swans that glide gracefully in the water. We have outfitted the bridge over the pond with seats so folks can sit and watch the water bird antics.

Our biggest birds are a pair of emus that look you right in the face with their huge, expressive eyes and eat out of your hand. They live beside the corral which houses pygmy goats and a llama called Dalai. Hence, the Dalai Llama lives here. In addition, Isis Oasis was, until recently, home to a living unicorn, who was offered to us by a friend. (He died at a very advanced age.) Oberon was a pygmy goat with a horn right in the middle of his forehead. He was very magical, and I used to tell guests that if they managed to touch his horn they could make a wish that would come true. Many have done so and hopefully, their wishes have materialized.

We have built many cat habitats for our ocelots, servals, bobcats, jungle cats and chausies (a hybrid of jungle cat and domestic cat). These were erected all around the old farmhouse that I live in. I love living in close proximity to them and visit them every day, bringing them treats. Several times a year, our breeding pairs have kittens. I then spend several months hand-feeding the babies so they will be tame. Since I cannot keep them all, I find them homes with people who have experience with exotic cats and a license to keep them. Some have become ambassador cats that go out in public to educate about the disappearing rain forests. The habitats of many species of wild cats are fast disappearing, while poaching continues in spite of it being outlawed. Ocelots are endangered, and I feel it is important to create more of them in the world. It seems to be one of my assignments in this lifetime. We have produced now seven generations of domestic-born ocelots.

Cats were sacred to the Goddess Isis and the ancient Egyptians worked with animals creating hybrids. They had serval cats and jungle cats. At Isis Oasis we have a combination of the two. We are calling it the Isis Cat. We are working toward mixing this with a domestic cat so it can make a legal pet for those who would enjoy having a large spotted cat with a really good personality.

I have become known as an expert on the ocelot, after breeding them for over thirty-five years. Alas, there are very few people doing this. I am very thankful I have been granted the ability and opportunity to love and raise these wonderful cats.

I have many cat stories, but that would be a whole new book. In fact, I have started writing it. The title is "Lots and Lots of Ocelots."

We feel honored that the Goddess has chosen us to help to add more of these beautiful species to the universe. Guests are always very pleased to visit our sanctuary of animals and birds for they have often never seen creatures that are so beautiful so close up.

When I was ordained as a Priestess of Isis the two other Goddesses I wished to serve were Bast, the cat Goddess of gentleness, and Sekhmet, the lion Goddess of strength. I have learned to call upon both of these feline Goddesses according to the situation in which I find myself,

The ancient Egyptians lived closely with their animals and often saw them as Goddesses and Gods. They worshipped them for their amazing attributes. Certainly just watching animals closely is always very impressive. They have much to teach us.

Today, we have so many restrictions it is not easy to live with anything other than domestic animals, though I hope the children of the future will have the opportunity to interact with animals of many kinds. Today, in order to keep the wild cats we have, we can be inspected at any time by the U.S. Department of Agriculture or the California Department of Fish and Game, both of which insist we maintain a license to have them. They impose a large fee each year to allow us to keep our beautiful family of cats

It is worth it, though, especially when we can enlighten children about ocelots and serval cats, both of which they have usually never heard of. We often take children on a tour of our habitats and they totally become enamored with the beauty of the cats and birds.

Through the animals we get to introduce the Goddess Isis to those who have never heard of her.

That is one of the purposes of Isis Oasis Sanctuary and we sometimes say we are on the front lines, for we are open to guests of many kinds and offer a tour of our animal habitats every Sunday. Since Isis is a Nature Goddess it is fitting that we have these sacred animals and birds on our land. This gives us the opportunity to tell many about the Temple of Isis and the word is spreading. Isis lives!

*Loreon with Pharaoh,
a very friendly ocelot*

Bobcat

A black and a white swan at the pond

Emu

The Isis Cat

Serval

Ocelot close up

Ocelot kitten

The TEMPLE of ISIS MANIFESTS

After the trip to Egypt and Greece, which had been quite strenuous, I went to see my heart doctor. To my surprise and alarm, he told me I had to have a bypass right away. This was certainly one of the most horrendously scary things I had ever faced. Since it had to be done to stay alive, I decided to make it into a kind of a ceremony.

The journey to the place of the open heart ceremony was cold and dark. The sun hadn't yet displayed itself. I went with Paul to the east wing of the local hospital and entered a room to be bathed by a young man with long hair. We got into a conversation about cats, wherein he disclosed his knowledge of Paganism. He was a perfect one to receive me and I thought of him as the God Bes, lightening things up with his humor and genuine warmth. He began to wheel me to the chambers of the place of the opening of the heart.

A lovely young nurse came up on one side of my gurney and introduced herself as my operating nurse, but I knew differently and designated her the Goddess Nepthys. Another appeared and said she was my other nurse, and she was even more beautiful than the first, I gave her the title of the Goddess Isis. In the theatre where the ceremony for the opening of the heart would begin, was the casual figure of the anesthetist who I transformed into Anubis forthwith. He took no time in putting me in a state of grace far from reality and where I would be guided into and through the underworld.

The surgeon, the one I called Thoth or Tehuti, must have been lurking in the shadows, for I never saw him, though I had met him briefly and felt trust in his professionalism. Soon I saw him in my mind's eye, bent over my body with his scalpel finely curved as the beak of a sacred ibis. I felt surrounded in white light with luminous gardens all around in colors that I had never known.

I awoke later in a room. It was noon and I was woozy with sleep. I felt as though I were in a netherworld unknown to me but filled with light and not unpleasant. Nurses came by and felt me, massaged me, and washed me, I must not use my arms in certain ways, as the operation included a practice called "the breaking open of the sternum." I had to carry a small pillow over the place where my sternum stuck out and was sore. A nurse played a video for me made up of beautiful nature visions, and great music put together in a gorgeous way. This was a true plus for ending the evening in my hospital bed. I had vivid dreams but they have faded from my memory.

For several days I lingered in this intensive care ward and slept a lot. When I was moved to a regular room, I was able to take a walk through the white corridor, though I got lost coming back. Some rooms were filled with anxious people, waiting to see if their loved ones would survive. When I did find my way back to my room I went to sleep only to be awakened by the night nurse, a handsome young man. He told me he had been to Egypt five times and showed interest in the book I had with me, *The Temple of the Cosmos*. He bore a remarkable resemblance to my nephew, Bruce, when he was younger. I wondered when Leslie my niece, would be visiting me, and perhaps Curtis, my cousin who called to say he was going to visit. Even Paul has not shown up. It was very peaceful.

I can see myself communing with my great tree, visualizing following my dreams. My life had been prolonged. The Goddess willed that I would undergo this and the reason will be revealed. I will not let the gift of life be taken lightly and will find a way to receive guidance and to proceed with wisdom and love.

There is nothing like a life threatening experience to move you in a new direction. My survival of the heart ceremony did just that. I knew I must inform Paul that he needed to make a change in his way of behaving. I knew that I would no longer be trampled by his periodic verbal abuse and that my mental and physical condition could no longer tolerate his fits of anger and negativity. It was clear that his drinking must cease to accomplish this turn-around in behavior. I wrote him a letter laying out a plan for us to part or possibly stay together if he could be sober.

How many women undergo this same problem? I began to realize that perhaps this was something I had to deal with in order to help others understand this dilemma. Men often have addictive behaviors. I seem to attract men who do. I began to see that with resolve and patience one can help alleviate the addiction and that can lead to peace.

Paul joined AA and our relationship began to improve. No longer would he rage and shout. No longer would I have to react to his negative behavior. Without alcohol as a contributing factor, our relationship began to thrive again and we stayed together. Sadly, after Paul became sober, he found he needed a hip replacement and then a second one. Then he found he had prostate cancer and started treatment.

Finally we discovered he needed a liver transplant and he was put on a long waiting list. He began to wither away and got very sick and shaky. One day we were in the city and I took him to the hospital, as he thought he had an appointment there. As it happened, he did not, but when we got there I pleaded for the doctor to see him. It was a long wait and Paul wanted to go home, but I insisted we stay, and when he saw the doctor it was clear he needed to be admitted to the hospital.

I drove home alone, wondering what would happen. Strangely, just then a liver was donated and Paul became the recipient. It was truly amazing, and in time he got better. The cancer shrunk, the liver took, the hips worked, and Paul became the really nice person he always was underneath his addiction and afflictions. We spent many precious days in each other's company.

One day Arisa, who had the Union Temple of Isis, visited and told me her life had changed a great deal. She and her partner had separated and she no longer had time to keep up her church, but she kept it alive on paper. I asked her, "How would you like to move it to Isis Oasis? We could take over and really work on keeping it alive." She thought it a good idea and I found myself now not only an arch priestess in the Fellowship of Isis, but the head of the Temple of Isis, a church recognized by the U.S. government and the state of California.

I discovered that many wish to be ordained and become a Priestess or Priest of Isis. We ask those wanting to become clergy to write a spiritual biography and point out what they are doing to offer service to the planet. Then, we send them their certificate and card designating them a Reverend in the Temple of Isis.

For me, it feels somewhat unnatural to have a church and to be in the position that I find myself. I really have no background for something like this, but the Goddess propelled me on. Every October we have a large convocation at Isis Oasis with Lady Olivia among us and other invited guests. It is then that many became ordained in both the Fellowship of Isis, which has thousands of members all over the world, and the Temple of Isis in Geyserville.

One of our Priestesses, Leema, a sacred dancer, held a workshop at Isis Oasis. As a result we met a couple from Virginia City, Nevada, Zarita and Warren. After that they came from afar many times to assist us in our efforts, for they worshipped the Goddess and had their own Temple of Isis. We even had the same license plates: TO ISIS. It was almost uncanny and we were quite delighted to have them assist us whenever they visited. Zarita was well-versed in ancient Egyptian lore and we enjoyed the same things. She was also a dancer, singer and actress and she and Warren would help us with the plays we put on each year. Little did we know the important role they would later assume...

There was a house that adjoined our property that I had always wanted to purchase, In addition to the original property and buildings, I had obtained the wonderful old house with redwood walls like the house we lived in, as well as a quaint one bedroom cottage and a tower, all of which needed major work.

I remember walking to the river before I decided on this possible purchase, saying to myself that I will find the answer on this walk as to whether or not to buy the property. The decision was difficult, for it was after my heart problems and I did not know how long I had to live. On a walk across the street, through a beautiful orchard to the river, I searched my mind for a decisive answer. Then, on the way back, right on the path, I spied a round red object. I picked it up and marveled at it, for there was no reason for it to be in the plum orchard at all. It was a tiny red tomato in perfect shape and in exactly the spot where I could look up and see the large house that I was considering adding to our center. I told myself that it was surely an omen that meant the purchase would be fruitful. This gave me the impetus to implement the purchase. It did prove to be positive even though the amount of work to get the buildings usable for our purposes was great.

But, illness takes its toll and we were growing old. We had to face our mortality. During this time of aging, I tried valiantly to carry on, even though I, too, was feeling the ravages of age. It was hard to persist, but we did.

The bed and breakfast business slowed down, for most people seem to want all the amenities of a major hotel. The retreat business slowed down also, due to the economy, and groups canceled often, lacking enough participants. We had less staff and had to do a lot of the work ourselves. Isis Oasis began to look a little sad and threadbare. Still, when things broke we fixed them and whatever the Oasis needed, we would supply.

When still another house adjoining finally came up for sale it was impossible for me to make a bid, for the work at Isis Oasis was all we could deal with. I wished that it could be bought by one of our clergy, for I imagined that we could have a community some day that would be similar to the one the Baha'i had there so long ago.

Then one day a man visited and announced he was our new neighbor. He and a partner bought the property for a bed and breakfast, but they wanted to have more land and wondered if we would sell part of our property. He wanted the other old house, cottage and tower and the field in which we had a huge yurt, a dome, a small yurt, a tipi, as well as a trailer and bathhouse. It was a hard decision, but I felt perhaps it was time to get smaller.

We agreed upon a price. I figured that if they bought the land and houses, it would be easier for us to manage the lodge, theatre, big kitchen and pavilion and our own house, along with the mobile homes and trailers for the staff. I imagined that we could use the money to fix everything up and do a lot less, for I was beginning to have a problem walking due to arthritis.

Around this time the fire department next door wanted a part of our property on the north side. Three quarters of an acre would do for them, and I agreed to sell. Then began a nightmare of legalese, but while this was going on we were able to rent the retreat house and the cottage to some tenants.

All of this was a little confusing and the year was quite a different one, dealing with lawyers, surveyors, and endless paper work. I rented the retreat house to four men who had been rehabilitated from drinking and drugs, and the cottage was rented to a wealthy young girl. I felt like a landlady, collecting rents monthly. The business of Isis Oasis I turned over to the Temple of Isis and became non-profit which seemed appropriate, having never gotten a profit from this business anyway.

As the year ended, the two men with the plans for their fancy B&B opted out. It was the time of 9-11, and their main partner decided not to be involved. So the property was now back in my lap. Then the young girl gave me notice that she was going to leave as she was moving to San Francisco.

Odd, how things seem destined at times, and this was one of those times. Zarita called, in tears. Her son, with whom they lived in Nevada, had become very ill and needed to relocate to a lower elevation. Zarita, her mother and Warren had nowhere to go, so I offered her the cottage. She and Warren could help us and her ninety-year-old mother could be with them. They accepted, and our lives began to merge.

With Zarita's help, we set about to improve the rooms in the Lodge, and with Warren's help, we began to improve the grounds. There was much to do and a plan began to take shape. We would give our tenants notice, for we decided to take over the Retreat House again to add to Isis Oasis and it needed a total remake.

We decided to call it the Nesu House, *nesu*

meaning "royal" in the ancient Egyptian language, and make the rooms reflect the lives of different famous queens of Egypt. There was Nefertiti in the loft, Cleopatra in the living room and library, Nefertari, and Ankhesenamon in the bedrooms and Queen Ti's Tea room off the kitchen. The tower, nearby became Queen Hatshepsut's obelisk. All of this materialized by finding statuary and pictures much of which was already in our little shop on the premises. Things also appeared at the local Salvation Army, a wonderful source of paraphernalia. We painted, where needed, for the walls were all a wonderful redwood as were the ceilings, and purchased some furnishings that suited the theme. It truly became a marvelous space for workshops once again.

The restoration of the Lodge was ongoing, also. The rooms were each redecorated to reflect the attributes of the twelve best-known Goddesses in the Egyptian pantheon. One of the walls in each room bore a color that most represented its Goddess, and decorative accouterments reflective of each Goddess were placed artistically throughout, Also, a description of each Goddess was displayed on the back of the doors of the rooms to make the stay of each person using them both enjoyable as well as educational. People visiting are amazed and often comment on the unique beauty of the rooms.

The exterior of the lodge has been painted a very tasty combination of colors: sand, brick, purple, and turquoise. Above the bay windows of the lounge, we placed the solar disk and wings. I had spoken about wanting a winged solar disk to put above some of the entryways, as they are always placed over the doors leading to the temples in Egypt. Shortly after this wish, a catalogue arrived with just such a piece and I ordered two. One came with a crack in it, so the company sent another. I repaired the crack and hung it inside the large living space at the Nesu house.

The plans to enhance Isis Oasis never seem to end. I often feel like Madame Winchester, who never stopped building on her mansion in San Jose, California.

Once, I put on a workshop for women where they were to sculpt a Goddess figure and put on its head a symbol that would represent them. Each Egyptian Goddess has a headdress: Isis has a throne, Selkhet has a scorpion, Neith has a spindle, Maat has a feather, and so on. Each meaningful object represents what that Goddess stood for. I choose a moth. I dabble in the dark, but am always attracted to the light. Like a moth, I am elusive and have flitted about trying different things. My feelers are ever ready to investigate some new experience. I appreciate the strength and beauty of the moth even over and above the butterflies that I used to collect with wonder and awe.

I find that Nature offers so much that one must be ever amazed that it all exists. Those who are bored with life need only to look around them, acknowledging that there is so much that Nature has provided for us. I see the Goddess Isis as Nature and worship her in that way. Her wonders never cease. We live in such a marvelous world that it is bizarre how we as a species do not preserve it as though it were a precious jewel. It seems incredible that we could even contemplate destroying each other and all the beautiful animals and birds that exist on the planet. We need to, as a species, be more appreciative and learn to love each other.

Each Sunday we present a ceremony, open to all, in the Grand Temple of Isis, which we create in the Theatre. Every week there is a different subject and I write a scroll of the week to encompass the theme. After being anointed, those that gather in the Temple begin by honoring the four directions. We have created a fabulous altar at the back of the Grand Temple. There are offerings of flowers, fruit, or feathers, in a bowl that those attending may bring to the altar with their prayers. We often discuss the forty-two Ideals of Maat. We find that living according to these simple principles give our lives a purposeful direction.

Sometimes we show a film or play some music, which we dance to, using our sistrums and drums to enhance the experience. Afterward, we enjoy having tea in our pavilion along with discussion. We imagine our congregation will grow as time goes on. I call this gathering "Sacred Sunday Salons."

Prior to the ceremony, we show our collection of animals and birds to those wishing to see them. We like to bring these wonders of nature to the attention of our guests. Many times there are baby ocelots or servals for them to admire. All are invited to get in touch with the gigantic fir tree which spreads over Isis Oasis. We believe that if you place your forehead in a special spot on that tree you will get zapped with good energy. We charge nothing for these services and hope to get donations that will sustain us as time goes on.

The fire department gave me a building that will make a wonderful art studio and gallery. I have kilns for making enamels and glass for making windows. There are lots of oil paints and canvases on easels. I am anxious to once again spend much of my time with a paintbrush or doing a craft. It is all in the plans. If one holds a thought, or even a dream, in time it will manifest. The trick is to focus!

After this building was complete, I determined to build a labyrinth beside it. I had looked at the space and imagined the labyrinth, then I pulled a Goddess card and got one that said "build a labyrinth." The next day, those working on the firehouse wanted to do something to help us since they had parked on our land while the building was going on. I asked them to flatten the area. Then I designed the labyrinth in the form of an *ankh*. A Priest of the Temple, who did architectural work on the computer, made plans and advised me about amounts of stone to use for this forty-two-foot circumference labyrinth. Then, a group came to stay who always offer us a 1/2 hour of work each for three days. Their assignment was to make the labyrinth. So, in only a week the labyrinth was done!

I advise people to walk it in a particular way. As you enter the ankh, you contemplate your life up to this point. When you reach the center there is a disk painted with an image of the Goddess Isis. I suggest walking around this seven times as the ancient Egyptians circumambulated their temples. On your way back out, I advise you to imagine how you would like your future life to be. I call this "the labyrinth manifestation," for, much like the meditation temple we built here, it came together so easily.

The Goddess has her own time, but as Lord Strathloch said, you must be receptive and be willing to meet her halfway. We have witnessed the way in which manifestation of dreams happens. We are planning to maintain this spiritual space, creating a kind of separate world that is in some way a replica of what the ancient Egyptians had strived for and maintained during good times in their long history.

Isis Oasis is destined to continue as a living memorial attesting to the fact that there really is a Goddess. The Goddess Isis is the embodiment of all Goddesses and encompasses them within her extended wings. We are here to keep her magical name alive, for it is imperative that she should never be forgotten.

When I was getting toward the end of writing my story, a profound thing happened. I opened the front door of my house, and there on the ledge of the door sat a Cecropian moth, the very same kind as the one I had watched hatch when I was six years old. I was quite amazed to find it there and also profoundly moved by its beauty, once again. I scooped it up in a container and took it to the butterfly garden where I photographed it before it flew away. I cannot imagine how this could have happened, as I had never seen another one before that early incident or afterwards. When looking it up on the internet, I discovered one is not likely to see them in the daytime at all, as they fly only at night. I wondered what kind of sign this might be and imagined it of a supernatural nature. How could it be otherwise?

This story could go on, for there is much that has happened and much that will yet happen, but with the appearance of the Cecropian moth, I realized it was perfect to end my story here. I do so now and I entreat you to summon the Goddess Isis to you and find out how she will help you to manifest your dreams.

As the ancient Egyptians said...BARAKA! meaning: " May your soul speak with your spirit!"

Goddess Bless,

Right Reverend Loreon Vigné

Loreon, age 73, in front of the Temple of Isis she built

The 42 IDEALS of MAAT

1. I honor virtue
2. I benefit with gratitude
3. I am peaceful
5. I affirm that all life is sacred
6. I give offerings that are genuine
7. I live in truth
8. I regard all altars with respect
9. I speak with sincerity
10. I consume only my fair share
11. I offer words of good intent
12. I honor animals as sacred
13. I relate in peace
14. I can be trusted
15. I care for the Earth
16. I keep my own council
17. I speak positively of others
18. I remain in balance with my emotions
19. I am trustful in relationships
20. I hold purity in high esteem
21. I spread joy
22. I do the best I can
23. I communicate with compassion
24. I listen to opposing opinions
25. I create harmony
26. I invoke laughter
27. I am open to love in various forms
28. I am forgiving

29. I am kind

30. I act respectfully of others

31. I am accepting

32. I follow my inner guidance

33. I speak with consideration of others

34. I do good

35. I give blessings

36. I keep the waters pure

37. I speak with optimism

38. I praise divinity

39. I am humble

40. I achieve with integrity

41. I advance through my own abilities

42. I embrace the all

Loreon was one of nine Priestesses of the Temple of Isis who traveled in Egypt in 1995 and undertook to rewrite these laws from the ancient text. Although each deals with the same subjects as the ancient ones, they were updated and made positive so we might utilize them today.

Recently we realized we did not like the word laws. It was too masculine, rigid, and linear. Ideals suited us more, for the Goddess way, is to be more open.

The ideals also are malleable and may change as even higher consciousness evolves. As an example the 2nd ideal "I benefit without violence" was changed to "I benefit with gratitude."

EPILOGUE

The Goddess is known to change everything she touches. After thinking I was finished with my biography, there were some major changes at Isis Oasis Sanctuary.

Zarita and Warren went back to Nevada because Warren had a stroke and could no longer help us. I had thought they would never leave and would take over after I could no longer run things here. There is a new and caring couple here now helping me keep things together with the aid of the Goddess.

Then Paul died. He was not feeling well and went into the hospital for tests and never came out. During a month in the hospital they literally killed him by injecting a drug that caused him to become comatose and unable to function on his own. They then put a feeding tube in the wrong place, causing him to get pneumonia. He died on Aug. 6 2005.

In September I held a memorial for him, where people from many parts of Paul's life came to speak of their special experiences with him. Many people loved Paul for his kindness and generosity. In a ceremony, we placed his ashes in the ground and planted a flowering crepe mayrtle tree over them.

Although Paul and I experienced many trials together, we also enjoyed many wonderful times with each other. I always advise our Priestesses to try to stay with their companions, since my own experience has shown me that there is a possibility of working things out so that both parties can be happy. It takes time and good intentions on both sides, but it can happen, and having a companion in your old age is definitely a plus.

Now, at age 73, I am alone once more. I have to assume that there is a reason for this, as the Goddess has a hand in it. We have a saying: What is, is. There is no looking back and from this point I must continue to move forward to see where her next assignment takes me.

Just before he entered the hospital, Paul gifted me with two large canvases and some brushes. I have taken that to mean that I must start painting again. I have determined to create an art gallery at Isis Oasis where I shall show the works of the clergy of the Temple as well as my own.

The day I went to pick up Paul's ashes at the crematorium, I went to the purple house in San Francisco to clean out our personal effects so I might rent the apartment. I opened the middle drawer of our old rolltop desk and in it I found this Native American prayer:

Do not stand at my grave and weep
I am not there. I do not sleep.
I am a thousand winds that blow.
I am the diamond glints on snow.
I am the sunlight on ripened grain.
I am the gentle Autumn rain.
When you awaken in the mornings, hush.
I am the swift up-flinging of
Quiet birds in circling flight.
I am the soft star that shines at night.
Do not stand at my grave and cry.
I am not there. I did not die.

While Paul was in his delirium at the hospital, he told me it was important to "get the certificates," and described them as being red with a blue border. I did not know at the time what he meant. At the crematorium, they gave me Paul's death certificate. It was red with a blue border.

Somehow Paul knew that his life would end and he could see beyond it. I know he is still guiding the Temple of Isis as the wonderful Priest he is.

Now there are many Priestesses and Priests to help support the Temple of Isis, so that it can continue after I, too, will have become a tree.

Goddess Bless.